Ajax in Oracle JDeveloper

T0223128

Deepak Vohra

Ajax in Oracle JDeveloper

 Springer

Deepak Vohra
dvohra09@yahoo.com

ISBN 978-3-540-77595-9   ISBN 978-3-540-77596-6 (eBook)

DOI 10.1007/978-3-540-77596-6

Library of Congress Control Number: 2008921926

Cover Design: KünkelLopka, Heidelberg

Printed on acid-free paper

9 8 7 6 5 4 3 2 1

springer.com

Preface

Asynchronous JavaScript and XML (Ajax or AJAX) is a web technique to transfer XML data between a browser and a server asynchronously. Ajax is a web technique, not a technology. Ajax is based on the JavaScript, DOM, and XMLHttpRequest technologies. The "A" in Ajax is for Asynchronous, which implies that the web page sending the Ajax request continues to be processed while the Ajax request is processed on the server and an Ajax response returned to the browser. The web page or sections in the web page get refreshed with the XML data in the Ajax response without posting the web page to the server. Without Ajax the complete web page had to be reloaded. Ajax has the following advantages over non-Ajax web applications.

1. Reduced response time and reduced server load as the complete web page is not reposted.
2. Reduced bandwidth of web applications as only data is transferred and the HTML format is applied in the browser.
3. Separation of data, format and style.

Motivation for this Book

A vast array of Ajax frameworks is available and it is often a dilemma as to which Ajax framework would be the most suitable. Ajaxian.com[1] conducted a survey on Ajax frameworks and found that 25% of Ajax developers would rather not use any framework and prefer to use XMLHttpRequest directly. Out of the frameworks that are used Prototype is the most commonly used, because Prototype reduces the JavaScript required in an Ajax application. PHP is the most commonly used server side language for Ajax, but Xajax, the most commonly used Ajax framework for PHP, is used by only 4% of Ajax developers. One of the reasons for not using an Ajax framework could be the non-availability of an integrated development environment (IDE) that integrates the Ajax

---

[1] Ajaxian.com-http://ajaxian.com/archives/ajaxiancom-2006-survey-results

frameworks with web applications and provides other web application development features such as support for Java Database Connectivity (JDBC) for developing an Ajax based web application.

Various Ajax plugins such as Googlipse, EchoStudio 2, Yet Another GWT Plugin, and Backbase are available for Eclipse, but these plugins are framework specific. Thus, a different plugin has to be installed if a different Ajax framework is required to be used. Also, Eclipse does not have a built-in support for JDBC and most Ajax applications are database based.

We have used Oracle JDeveloper for Ajax, because JDeveloper has the following advantages over Eclipse.

1. JDeveloper 11g provides an integrated JavaScript Editor for Ajax/Web development.
2. JDeveloper provides a PHP extension, which may be used to develop Ajax applications with PHP; PHP being one of the most commonly used scripting languages on the web.
3. JDeveloper supports JSF. JSF GUI components may be selected from a JSF Component Palette and added to an Ajax web application.
4. JDeveloper has a built-in support for JDBC, which is a requirement for database based Ajax applications.
5. JDeveloper includes an embedded application server, the Oracle Container for Java EE (OC4J) server. JDeveloper also has the provision to connect to and deploy applications to any of the commonly used application servers such as Oracle Application Server, JBoss application server, and WebLogic Server.

While a number of books have been published on Ajax, none of the books is IDE based. Also, no other book on Ajax covers web search and RSS Feed with Ajax.

Who Should Read this Book?

The target audience of the book is Ajax developers. The target audience is also students taking a course in Ajax. The book discusses using Ajax in Oracle JDeveloper. If the reader is an Ajax developer, JDeveloper provides an integrated development environment for Ajax development. If the reader is already using JDeveloper for web development the book introduces the reader to adding Ajax to web applications. We have discussed the Prototype framework, the most commonly used Ajax framework. If the reader uses Ajax for dynamic form validation, the book covers dynamic form validation with Ajax frameworks for Java, JSP, JSF, and PHP. We have discussed Google AJAX Search API and Yahoo Web Services to add Ajax to web search. Ajax developers shall learn about setting the environment for developing various Ajax based applications and the procedure to develop Ajax based applications. Example applications are provided that may be modified to suit a developer's requirements. Chapters include illustrations at milestone stages of application development.

Outline to the Book Structure

In Chapter 1 we introduce the XMLHttpRequest object, which forms the basis of Ajax. We discuss the XMLHttpRequest properties and methods and also discuss the procedure to send an Ajax request and process the Ajax response. The integrated JavaScript Editor in JDeveloper 11g is also discussed.

In Chapter 2 we create an Ajax web application in JDeveloper 11g. We create an Ajax web application for dynamic form validation using a HTTP Servlet on the server-side in JDeveloper 11g. The example form used creates a catalog entry in Oracle database. Thus, the JDBC aspect of an Ajax application is also discussed. JDeveloper provides built-in support for JDBC with any database.

Chapter 3 discusses the Prototype JavaScript framework for Ajax. According to the Ajaxian.com survey Prototype is the most commonly used Ajax framework and is used by 43% of Ajax developers. Prototype reduces the JavaScript required in an Ajax application with JavaScript utility functions. The same Ajax application that is created in Chap. 2 is created with Prototype in JDeveloper 11g.

In Chapter 4 we create an Ajax application with Java on the server-side using the Google Web Toolkit (GWT) framework for Ajax. We integrate GWT in JDeveloper 11g by creating a run configuration for GWT Shell and Compiler. GWT versions 1.3 and later are licensed by Apache 2.0 open source.

In Chapter 5 we discuss Direct Web Remoting (DWR), another open source Ajax framework for Java. According to the Ajaxian.com survey DWR is used by 12% of Ajax developers. We create the database based dynamic form validation application with DWR in JDeveloper 11g.

In Chapter 6 we discuss AjaxTags Ajax framework for Java Server Pages (JSP). Prototype reduces JavaScript, and AjaxTags eliminates

JavaScript with JSP tag library tags. We integrate the AjaxTags tag library in JDeveloper 11g to create the same dynamic form validation application.

In Chapter 7 we discuss Ajax4jsf, an Ajax framework for JSF. JDeveloper provides an integrated support for JSF Core and HTML components using which we create a database based dynamic form validation application.

In Chapter 8 we discuss the PHP extension for JDeveloper 10g for creating a database based dynamic form validation application with PHP on the server-side. According to the Ajaxian.com survey PHP is the most commonly used platform for Ajax. JDeveloper 11g does not yet provide a PHP extension, therefore, we have used JDeveloper 10g in this chapter. Xajax, a PHP Ajax framework is used for generating the required JavaScript for the PHP Ajax application.

In Chapter 9 we discuss the Google AJAX Feed API to retrieve RSS 2.0 feed in a web application in JDeveloper 11g.

In Chapter 10 we discuss adding Ajax to web search with Google AJAX Search API and Yahoo Web Services. We discuss localized web search using the Google AJAX Search API and contextual web search using Yahoo Web Services.

Prerequisite Skills

It is not a goal to instruct the reader about JavaScript. Familiarity with JavaScript is required, and if the reader is not very familiar with JavaScript, the Netscape JavaScript Guide[2] would be a suitable reference. Also, it is assumed the reader has used Java, JSF, and PHP. Although we have discussed setting the environment in JDeveloper for Ajax, some familiarity with JDeveloper is also required.

Acknowledgements

The author would like to thank Hermann Engesser, Executive Editor Computer Science, Springer. Thanks are also due to Gabriele Fischer, the project manager at Springer, and to Michael Reinfarth, Production Editor, LE-TeX Jelonek.

---

[2]Netscape JavaScript Guide-http://wp.netscape.com/eng/mozilla/3.0/handbook/
   javascript/

About the Author

Deepak Vohra is a Sun Certified Java Programmer and Sun Certified Web Component Developer. He has a Master of Science in mechanical engineering from Southern Illinois University, Carbondale. Deepak is an Oracle Certified Associate. Moreover, he is a Manning Publications Technical editor and edited the Prototype and Scriptaculous in Action book.

Contents

1 What is Ajax?

1.1 Introduction

Asynchronous JavaScript and XML (Ajax) is a term for the process of transferring data between a client script and the server. The advantage of this is that it provides developers with a way to retrieve content from a Web server without reposting the page the user is currently viewing to the server. In concert with modern browsers' ability to dynamically change displayed content through programming code (JavaScript) that accesses the browser's DOM, Ajax lets developers update the HTML content displayed in the browser without refreshing the page. Thus, Ajax provides dynamic interaction between a client and a server. In other words, Ajax can make browser-based applications more interactive, more responsive, and more like traditional desktop applications. Google's Gmail and Outlook Express are two familiar examples that use Ajax techniques. Ajax has various applications, some of which are discussed below.

1. Dynamic Form Data Validation. As an example, suppose a user fills out a form to register with a web site.The validity of data in the form is not checked till the form is submitted. With Ajax, the data added to the form is dynamically validated using business logic in a server application. Thus, a complete form does not have to be posted to the server to check if data in the form is valid.
2. Auto completion. As a user adds some data to a form, the remaining form gets auto completed.
3. Refreshing data on a page. Some web pages require that data be refreshed frequently, a weather web site for example. Using the Ajax technique, a web page may poll the server for latest data and refresh the web page without reloading the page.

Ajax is based on XMLHttpRequest, JavaScript and XML DOM technologies. JavaScript and XML DOM technologies are relatively old technologies. Therefore we won't discuss these. XMLHttpRequest is a relatively new technology. In the next section, we shall discuss the XMLHttpRequest technology.

1.2 What is XMLHttpRequest?

Ajax takes advantage of an object built into all modern browsers-the XMLHttpRequest object-to send and receive HTTP requests and responses. An HTTP request sent via the XMLHttpRequest object does not require the page to have or post a <form> element. The "A" in Ajax stands for "asynchronous", which means that the XMLHttpRequest object's send() method returns immediately, letting the browser processing of other HTML/JavaScript on the Web page continue while the server processes the HTTP request and sends the response. While asynchronous requests are the default, the reader can optionally send synchronous requests, which halt other Web page processing until the page receives the server's response.

Microsoft introduced the XMLHttpRequest object as an ActiveX object in Internet Explorer (IE) 5. Other browser manufacturers, recognizing the object's utility, implemented the XMLHttpRequest object in their browsers, but as a native JavaScript object rather than as an ActiveX object. In turn, recognizing the value and security in that implementation type, Microsoft has recast the XMLHttpRequest in IE 7 as a window object property. Even when the implementation (and thus invocation) details differ, all the browsers' implementations have similar functionality and essentially identical methods. The W3C is working to standardize the XMLHttpRequest object, releasing a working draft of the W3C specification[1].

This chapter discusses the XMLHttpRequest object API in detail, listing and explaining all the properties and methods.

1.3 XMLHttpRequest Object Properties

The XMLHttpRequest object exposes various properties, methods, and events so Ajax scripts can process and control HTTP requests and responses. The rest of this chapter discusses these in detail.

---

[1] W3C XMLHttpRequest Specification- http://www.w3.org/TR/ XMLHttpRequest/

1.3.1 The readyState Property

The XMLHttpRequest object cycles through several states as it sends an HTTP request to the server, waits while the request is processed, and when it receives a response. So that scripts can respond appropriately to the various states, the object exposes a readyState property that represents the object's current state, as shown in Table 1.1.

Table 1.1 ReadyState Property Values

ReadyState Property Value	Description
0	Represents an "uninitialized" state in which an XMLHttpRequest object has been created, but not initialized.
1	Represents a "sent" state in which code has called the XMLHttpRequest open() method and the XMLHttpRequest is ready to send a request to the server.
2	Represents a "sent" state in which a request has been sent to the server with the send() method, but a response has not yet been received.
3	Represents a "receiving" state in which the HTTP response headers have been received, but message body has not yet been completely received.
4	Represents a "loaded" state in which the response has been completely received.

1.3.2 The onreadystatechange Property

The XMLHttpRequest object generates a readystatechange event whenever the readyState value changes. The onreadystatechange property accepts an EventListener value, specifying the method that the object will invoke whenever the readyState value changes.

1.3.3 The responseText Property

The responseText property contains the text of the HTTP response received by the client. When the readyState value is 0, 1, or 2 responseText contains an empty string. When the readyState value is 3 (Receiving), the response contains the incomplete response received by the client. When `readyState` is 4 (Loaded) the `responseText` contains the complete response.

1.3.4 The responseXML Property

The `responseXML` property represents the XML response when the complete HTTP response has been received (when `readyState` is 4), when the Content-Type header specifies the MIME (media) type as `text/xml`, `application/xml`, or ends in +xml. If the Content-Type header does not contain one of these media types, the `responseXML` value is `null`. The `responseXML` value is also `null` whenever the `readyState` value contains any value other than 4. The `responseXML` property value is an object of type `Document` interface, and represents the parsed document. If the document cannot be parsed (for example if the document is malformed or the character encoding of the document is not supported) the `responseXML` value is `null`.

1.3.5 The status Property

The `status` property represents the HTTP status code[2] and is of type `short`. The status attribute is available only when the `readyState` value is 3 (Receiving) or 4 (Loaded). Attempting to access the `status` value when `readyState` is less than 3 raises an exception.

1.3.6 The statusText Property

The `statusText` attribute represents the HTTP status code text and is also available only when the `readyState` value is 3 or 4. Attempting to access the `statusText` property for other `readyState` values raises an exception.

---

[2] Status Code Definitions- http://www.w3.org/Protocols/rfc2616/rfc2616-sec10.html

1.4 XMLHttpRequest Object Methods

The XMLHttpRequest object provides various methods to initiate and process HTTP requests, which are discussed in detail in the following sections.

1.4.1 The abort() Method

The abort() method is used to halt the HTTP request associated with an XMLHttpRequest object to reset the object to the uninitialized state.

1.4.2 The open() Method

The open(DOMString method, DOMString uri, boolean async, DOMString username, DOMString password) method is called to initialize an XMLHttpRequest object. The method parameter is required and specifies the HTTP method (GET, POST, PUT, DELETE, or HEAD) that want to use to send the request. To send data to the server, use the POST method. To retrieve data from the server, use the GET method. The uri parameter specifies the server URI to which the XMLHttpRequest object sends the request. The uri resolves to an absolute URI using the window.document.baseURI property—in other words, relative URIs will be resolved in the same way that the browser resolves relative URIs. The async parameter specifies whether the request is asynchronous; the default value is true. To send a synchronous request, set the parameter to false. For servers that require authentication, the optional username and password parameters may be supplied. After calling the open() method, the XMLHttpRequest objects sets its readyState property to 1 (Open) and resets the responseText, responseXML, status, and statusText properties to their initial values. It also resets the request headers. Note that the object resets these values if the open() method when readyState is 4.

1.4.3 The send() Method

After preparing a request by calling the open() method, the request is sent to the server. The send() method may be called only when the readyState value is 1, otherwise the XMLHttpRequest object raises an exception. The request gets sent to the server using the parameters supplied to the open() method. The send() method returns immediately when the async parameter is true, letting other client script processing   continue. The XMLHttpRequest object sets the readyState value to 2 (Sent) after the send() method has been called. When the server responds, before receiving the message body, if any,   the   XMLHttpRequest   object   sets   readyState   to 3 (Receiving). When the request has completed loading it sets readyState to 4 (Loaded). For a request of type HEAD, it sets the readyState value to 4 immediately after setting it to 3.

The send() method takes an optional parameter that may contain data of varying types. Typically, this method is used to send data to the server using the POST method. The send() method may be explicitly invoked with null, which is the same as invoking it with no argument. For most other   data   types,   set   the   Content-Type   header   using   the setRequestHeader() method (explained below) before invoking the send() method. If the data parameter in the send(data) method is of type DOMString, encode the data as UTF-8. If data is of type Document, serialize the data using the encoding specified by data.xmlEncoding, if supported or UTF-8 otherwise.

1.4.4 The setRequestHeader() Method

The setRequestHeader(DOMString   header,   DOMString value) method sets request headers. This method may be called after calling the open() method-when the readyState value is 1-otherwise you'll get an exception.

1.4.5 The getResponseHeader() Method

The   getResponseHeader(DOMString   header,   value) method   method is used to retrieve response header values. Call getResponseHeader() only when the readyState value is 3 or 4 (in other words, after the response headers are available); otherwise, the method returns an empty string.

1.4.6 The getAllResponseHeaders() Method

The getAllResponseHeaders() method returns all the response headers as a single string with each header on a separate line. The method returns null if readyState value is not 3 or 4.

1.5 Sending an Ajax Request

In Ajax, many requests that use the XMLHttpRequest are initiated from a HTML Event such as a button click (onclick) or a key press (onkeypress) that invokes a JavaScript function. Ajax has various applications including form validation. Sometimes a unique form field is required to be validated before the rest of the form may be filled. For example a registration form that requires a unique UserID. Without validation of the UserID field with Ajax the complete form would have to be filled and submitted. If the UserID is not valid, the form would have to be re-submitted. For example, a form field for a Catalog ID that must be validated on the server might be specified as follows.

```
<form name="validationForm" action="validateForm"
method="post">
   <table>
   <tr><td>Catalog Id:</td>
     <td>
      <input type="text"
         size="20"
         id="catalogId"
         name="catalogId"
         onkeyup="sendRequest()">
    </td>
    <td><div id="validationMessage"></div></td>
   </tr>
   </table></form>
```

The preceding HTML uses the validationMessage div to display a validation message for the input field Catalog Id. The onkeyup event invokes a JavaScript sendRequest() function. The sendRequest() function creates an XMLHttpRequest object. The process of creating an XMLHttpRequest object differs depending on the browser implementation. If the browser supports the XMLHttpRequest object as a window property (all common browsers do except IE 5 and 6), the code can call the XMLHttpRequest constructor. If the browser implements the XMLHttpRequest object as an ActiveXObject object (as in IE versions 5 and 6), the code uses the ActiveXObject constructor. The function below calls an init() function, which checks to determine the appropriate creation method to use before creating and returning the object.

```
<script type="text/javascript">
   function sendRequest(){
      var xmlHttpReq=init();
```

```
function init(){
  if (window.XMLHttpRequest) {
      return new XMLHttpRequest();
  }
  else if (window.ActiveXObject) {
    return new ActiveXObject("Microsoft.XMLHTTP");
  }}
</script>
```

Next, we need to initialize the XMLHttpRequest object using the open() method, specifying the HTTP method and the server URL to use.

```
var catalogId=encodeURIComponent(
    document.getElementById("catalogId").value);
  xmlHttpReq.open("GET", "validateForm?catalogId=" +
    catalogId, true);
```

HTTP requests sent with XMLHttpRequest are asynchronous by default, but the async parameter may be explicitly set to true as shown above.

In this case, the call to the URL validateForm invokes a servlet on the server-side, but it should recognized that the server-side technology is immaterial; the URL might actually be an ASP, ASP.NET, or PHP page, or a Web service—it doesn't matter as long as the page returns a response indicating whether the CatalogID value is valid. Because you're making an asynchronous call, we need to register a callback event handler that the XMLHttpRequest object will invoke when its readyState value changes. Remember that a change to the readyState value generates a readystatechange event. We register the callback event handler using the onreadystatechange property.

```
xmlHttpReq.onreadystatechange=processRequest;
```

Next, we need to send the request using the send() method. Because this request uses the HTTP GET method, the send() method may be invoked without an argument or null argument.

```
xmlHttpReq.send(null);
```

1.6 Processing an Ajax Request

In this example, because the HTTP method is GET, the receiving servlet on the server invokes a doGet() method, which retrieves the catalogId parameter value specified in the URL, and checks its validity against a database. The servlet needs to construct a response to be sent to the client.

This example returns XML, so it sets the HTTP content type of the response to text/xml and the Cache-Control header to no-cache. Setting the cache-control header prevents the browser from simply reloading the page from the cache.

```
public void doGet(HttpServletRequest request,
        HttpServletResponse response)
        throws ServletException, IOException {
        ...
        ...
        response.setContentType("text/xml");
        response.setHeader("Cache-Control", "no-
cache");
    }
```

The response from the server is an XML DOM object. Create an XML string that contains instructions to be processed on the client side. The XML string must have a root element.

```
out.println("<catalogId>valid</catalogId>");
```

The XMLHttpRequest object is designed to handle responses consisting of plain text or XML; but a response may be of another type if the user agent (UA) supports the content type.

The XMLHttpRequest object calls the event handler registered with onreadystatechange when the request state changes. Therefore, your event handler should check the readyState value and the HTTP status before processing the response. When the request has completed loading, which corresponds to readyState value 4, and the HTTP status is "OK", the response has completed, and we may invoke a JavaScript function to process the response content. The following script checks the values and invokes a processResponse() method when the response is complete.

```
function processRequest(){
        if(xmlHttpReq.readyState==4){
            if(xmlHttpReq.status==200){
                processResponse();
            }
        }
    }
```

The processResponse() method uses the XMLHttpRequest objects' responseXML and responseText properties to retrieve the HTTP response. As explained above, the responseXML is available only if the media type of the response is text/xml, application/xml or ends in +xml. The responseText property returns the response as plain text. For an XML response we would retrieve the content as follows.

```
var msg=xmlHttpReq.responseXML;
```

With the XML stored in the *msg* variable, we retrieve the element's value using the DOM method getElementsByTagName().

```
var catalogId=msg.getElementsByTagName(
     "catalogId")[0].firstChild.nodeValue;
```

Finally, we test the element value to create a message that we display by updating the HTML content of the validationMessage div on the Web page, using the innerHTML property.

```
if(catalogId=="valid"){
     var validationMessage =

document.getElementById("validationMessage");
     validationMessage.innerHTML = "Catalog Id is
Valid";
     }
   else
   {
       var validationMessage =

document.getElementById("validationMessage");
     validationMessage.innerHTML = "Catalog Id is
not Valid";
     }
```

That's the full cycle. The XMLHttpRequest object provides dynamic interaction between a client and a server by transferring data without posting the Web page to the server. We use JavaScript to launch a request and process the return value, and then we use browser DOM methods to update data on the page. We are using Oracle JDeveloper 11g IDE for Ajax, because JDeveloper 11g provides an integrated JavaScript Editor for Ajax/web development. We shall discuss the JavaScript Editor next.

1.7 JDeveloper Integrated JavaScript Editor

JDeveloper 11g includes an integrated JavaScript editor for creating JavaScript. In a JDeveloper web application JavaScript may be added directly to a JSP file, but the JavaScript may also be created in a separate .js file and the .js file added to the JSP using the <script/> tag.

Creating the JavaScript file separately has an advantage as the integrated JavaScript Editor may be availed of. Create a JavaScript file by selecting **File>New** and in the **New Gallery** window **Web Tier>HTML>JavaScript File**. Copy some JavaScript code to the JavaScript file. Create a JSP file to add the JavaScript file to with **File>New**. In the **New Gallery** window select **Web Tier>JSP** in **Categories** and select **JSP** in **Items**. The JavaScript file and the JSP file are shown in Fig. 1.1.

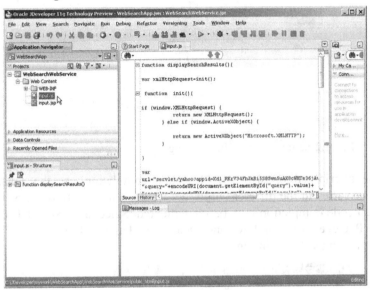

Fig. 1.1 JavaScript File

One of the features of the JavaScript editor is syntax highlighting. To add syntax highlighting select **Tools>Preferences** and in the **Preferences** window select **Code Editor>Syntax Colors**. Select **JavaScript** in the **Language** list. The **Font Style**, **Foreground** color and **Background** color may be set for the different JavaScript constructs in the **Syntax Colors** window as shown in Fig. 1.2.

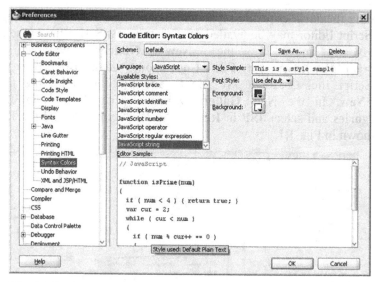

Fig. 1.2 Setting Syntax Highlighting

JavaScript editor also provides code completion. As the JavaScript syntax varies in the different browsers we need to specify the browser for which code completion is to be implemented. Select **JavaScript Editor** in the **Preferences** window and select a **Target Browser** for code completion as shown in Fig. 1.3.

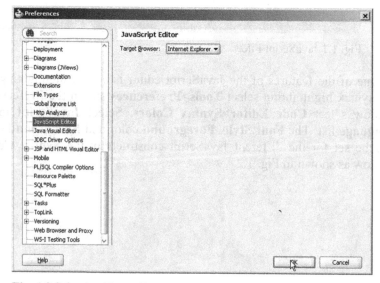

Fig. 1.3 Selecting Target Browser

In the JavaScript file right-click and select **Source>Completion Insight** or **Source>Smart Completion Insight** for code insight as shown in Fig. 1.4.

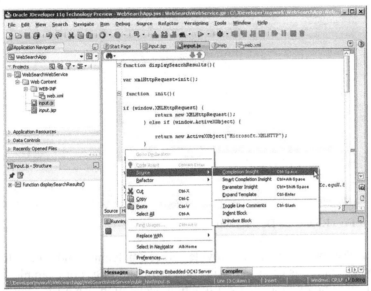

Fig. 1.4 Using Code Insight

Another feature of the JavaScript editor is **Go To Declaration** using which a JavaScript variable or function may be navigated to from a usage of the JavaScript variable/function. For example, select a usage of the variable xmlHttpRequest, right-click and select **Go To Declaration** to go to the declaration of the xmlHttpRequest variable as shown in Fig. 1.5.

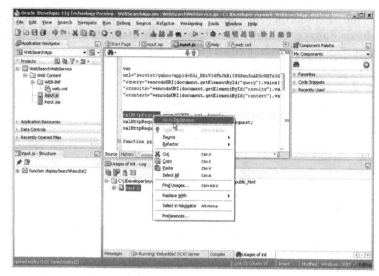

Fig. 1.5 Go To Declaration

JavaScript editor also provide brace matching and code folding. Another feature is error underling and error auditing. For example, add an error by removing the '{' for a function declaration. An error analysis gets run and the errors get underlined as shown in Fig. 1.6.

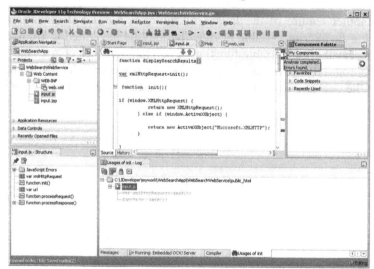

Fig. 1.6 Error Analysis

Usages of a variable or function may be retrieved by selecting the variable/function and selecting **Find Usages**. For example, select `xmlHttpRequest`, right-click and select **Find Usages**. The usages of the `xmlHttpRequest` variable get listed in the log window as shown in Fig. 1.7.

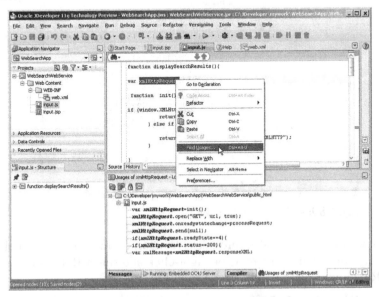

Fig. 1.7 Find Usages

A JavaScript file is integrated with the **Structure** pane from which different variables and functions may be navigated to as shown in Fig. 1.8.

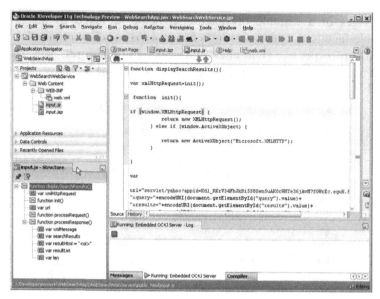

Fig. 1.8 JavaScript File Structure

JavaScript editor also provides refactoring to rename or delete a variable or function. To refactor, right-click and select **Refactor>Rename** or **Refactor>Delete Safely** as shown in Fig. 1.9.

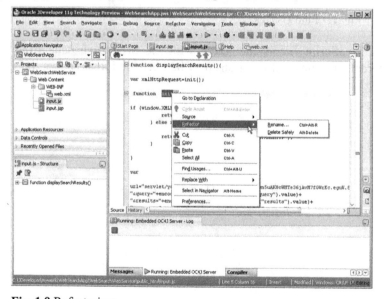

Fig. 1.9 Refactoring

To add the JavaScript file to a JSP drag and drop the file from the Application navigator to the JSP. A `<script/>` element for the JavaScript file gets added to the JSP as shown in Fig. 1.10.

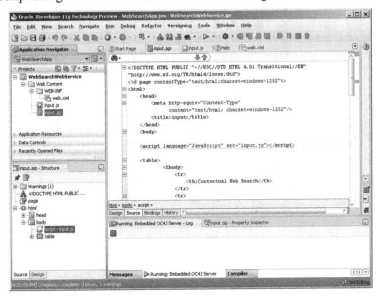

Fig. 1.10 Adding JavaScript to JSP

1.8 Summary

In this chapter we discussed the XMLHttpRequest object, which forms the basis of Ajax. An Ajax request is initiated from a browser by first creating an XMLHttpRequest object and opening the XMLHttpRequest object using the open() method. The method used to create the XMLHttpRequest varies with the browser used. An Ajax request is sent using the send() method of XMLHttpRequest. When the request completes the Ajax XML response is retrieved using the responseXML attribute of the XMLHttpRequest object. The web page that sent the Ajax request is updated with the Ajax XML response by retrieving the XML data and setting the data into the web page elements using DOM functions. We also discussed the JavaScript Editor integrated into JDeveloper 11g.

2 Developing an Ajax Web Application

2.1 Introduction

As we discussed in the previous chapter Asynchronous JavaScript for XML (Ajax) is a web technique that combines JavaScript, Document Object Mode (DOM) and XMLHttpRequest technologies to provide dynamic interaction between a client and a server. Ajax is a technique, not a technology. As an example, suppose a user fills out a form to add data to a database table. Without Ajax, the validity of data in the form is not checked till the form is submitted. With Ajax, the data added to the form is dynamically validated as the data is added to form fields using business logic in a server side application. Thus, a complete form does not have to be posted to the server to check if data added in the form is valid. In this chapter we shall create a web application using Ajax in JDeveloper 11g to validate an input form.

2.2 Setting the Environment

Install JDeveloper 11g[1] if not already installed. To install JDeveloper 11g download the zip file for JDeveloper 11g and unzip the zip file to the *C:/JDeveloper11g* directory. The preconfigured paths in JDeveloper 11g require that JDeveloper be installed in the JDeveloper11g directory. First, create a JDeveloper application and project with **File>New**. In the **New Gallery** window select **General** in **Categories** and Application in **Items**. Click on **OK**. In the **Create Application** window specify the **Application Name** and click on **OK**. In the **Create Project** window specify the **Project Name** and click on **OK**. A JDeveloper application and project get added to **Application Navigator** as shown in Fig. 2.1.

---

[1]JDeveloper11g-http://www.oracle.com/technology/software/products/ jdev/htdocs/soft11tp.html

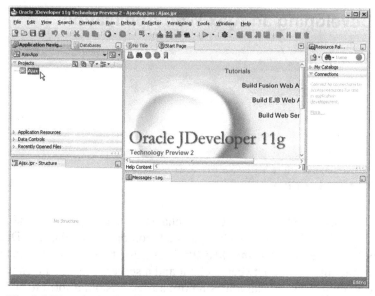

Fig. 2.1 JDeveloper Application and Project

In the project add a JSP file, *input.jsp*, with **File>New**. In the **New Gallery** window select **Web Tier>JSP** in **Categories** and **JSP** in **Items** as shown in Fig. 2.2. Click on **OK**.

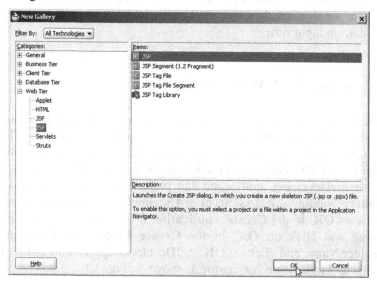

Fig. 2.2 Creating a JSP

In the **JSP File** window specify a file name and click on **OK**. JSP *input.jsp* gets added to **Application Navigator** as shown in Fig. 2.3.

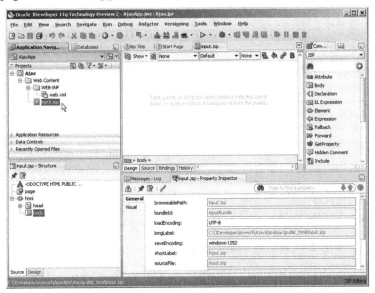

Fig. 2.3 New JSP in Application Navigator

The *input.jsp* JSP provides the client side of the Ajax web application. Similarly, add JSPs *catalog.jsp* and *error.jsp* for redirecting client application based on if the Ajax web application generates an error in creating a catalog entry. Next, create a JavaScript file *input.js* with **File>New**. In the **New Gallery** window select **Web Tier>HTML** in **Categories** and **JavaScript File** in **Items** and click on **OK** as shown in Fig. 2.4.

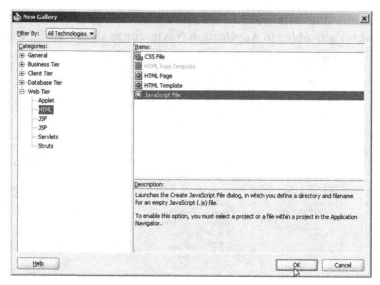

Fig. 2.4 Creating a JavaScript File

In the **Create JavaScript File** window specify **File Name** as *input.js* and click on **OK**. JavaScript file *input.js* gets added to **Application Navigator**. For server side processing, add a HTTP Servlet with **File>New**. In the **New Gallery** window select **Web Tier>Servlets** in **Categories** and **HTTP Servlet** in **Items** and click on **OK** as in Fig. 2.5.

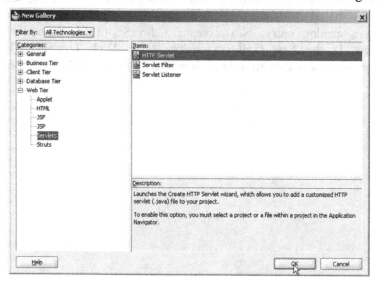

Fig. 2.5 Creating a Servlet

Click on **Next** in **Create HTTP Servlet Wizard**. In **Servlet Information** window, specify a Servlet name, `FormValidationServlet`, and click on **Next** as shown in Fig. 2.6.

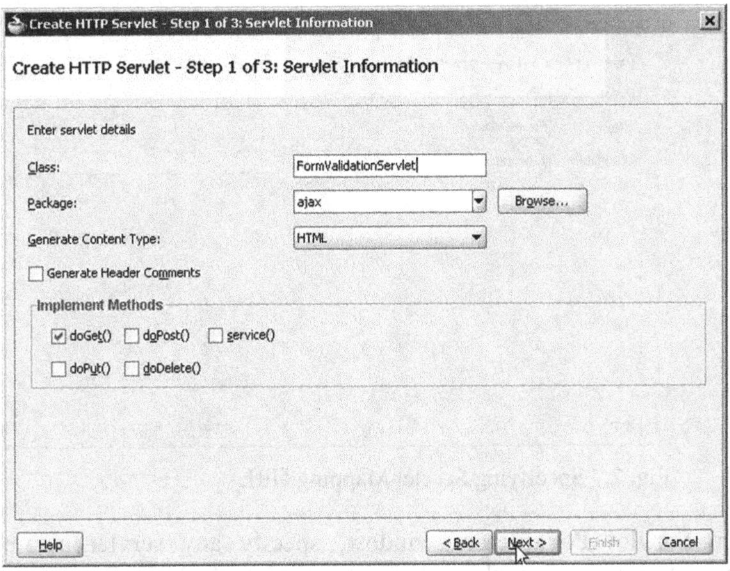

Fig. 2.6 Specifying Servlet Class

In the **Mapping Information** window specify a servlet mapping URL, `/validateForm` for example, and click on **Next** as shown in Fig. 2.7.

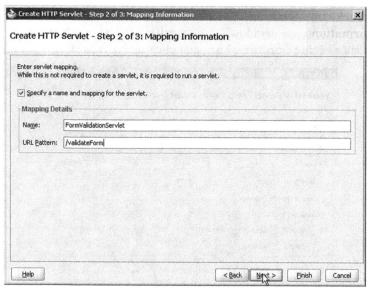

Fig. 2.7 Specifying Servlet Mapping URL

In **Servlet Parameters** window, specify any servlet parameters if required (none by default) and click on **Finish**. A HTTP Servlet gets added to the **Application Navigator**. Ajax web application structure is shown in Fig. 2.8.

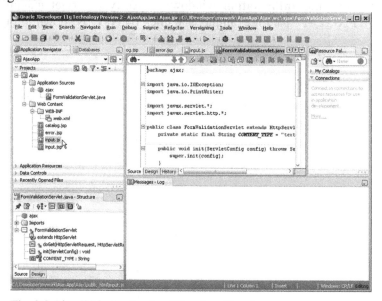

Fig. 2.8 Ajax Web Application Directory Structure

Next, add some required libraries to the Ajax project with **Tools>Project Properties**. In the **Project Properties** window select **Libraries and Classpath** and click on **Add Library**. Add library **Oracle JDBC**, which is required for Oracle database access. Click on **OK** in **Project Properties** window as shown in Fig. 2.9.

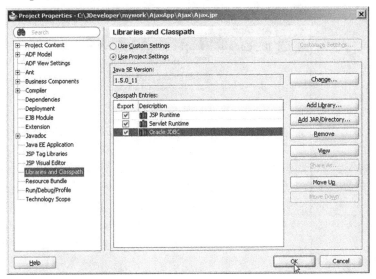

Fig. 2.9 Adding a Library

The Ajax web application in this chapter retrieves data and updates data in an Oracle database table. Install Oracle 10g database including the sample schemas and a database instance ORCL. Create a database table with SQL script listed below using SQL client SQL Plus or in command line.

```
CREATE    TABLE    OE.Catalog(CatalogId    VARCHAR(25),
Journal VARCHAR(25), Publisher Varchar(25), Edition
VARCHAR(25), Title Varchar(45), Author Varchar(25));
INSERT  INTO  OE.Catalog  VALUES('catalog1',  'Oracle
Magazine',   'Oracle  Publishing',  'Nov-Dec  2004',
'Database Resource Manager
', 'Kimberly Floss');
INSERT  INTO  OE.Catalog  VALUES('catalog2',  'Oracle
Magazine',   'Oracle  Publishing',  'Nov-Dec  2004',
'From ADF UIX to JSF', 'Jonas Jacobi');
INSERT  INTO  OE.Catalog  VALUES('catalog3',  'Oracle
Magazine',    'Oracle   Publishing',   'March-April
2005', 'Starting with Oracle ADF ', 'Steve Muench');
```

Next, define a JDBC Connection with the Oracle database in the **Databases** window. To create a JDBC connection, right-click on the **IDE Connections** node and select **New Connection** as shown in Fig. 2.10.

Fig. 2.10 Creating New Connection

The **Create Database Connection** wizard gets started. Specify a **Connection Name** and select the default **Connection Type**, **Oracle (JDBC)**. Specify **Username** as OE, because the database table was created in OE schema, and specify the Password for OE schema. In the **Oracle JDBC Settings** header, select the **thin** Driver, specify **Host Name** as localhost, and **JDBC Port** as 1521. Specify the **SID** as ORCL. Click on **Test Connection**. If a JDBC connection gets established a "Success" message gets displayed. Click on **OK** as shown in Fig. 2.11.

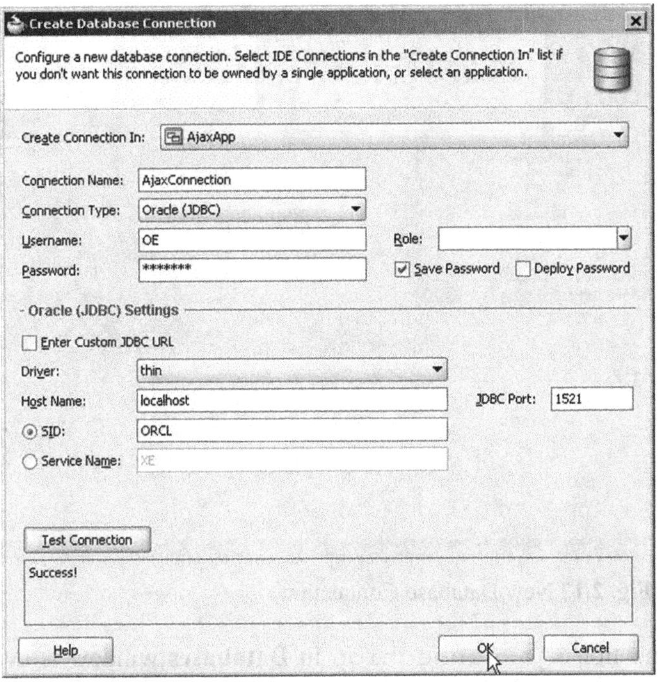

Fig. 2.11 Configuring a Connection

A node for the connection gets added to **IDE Connections** node in **Databases** window as shown in Fig. 2.12. The Catalog table may be modified if required using the **SQL Worksheet**.

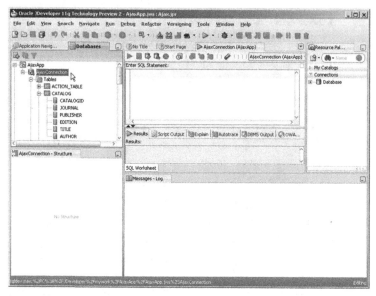

Fig. 2.12 New Database Connection

Connection `AjaxConnection` in **Databases** window is available as datasource with JNDI name `jdbc/AjaxConnectionDS`. To the `web.xml` configuration file we need to add the following `<resource-ref/>` element.

```
<resource-ref>
  <res-ref-name>jdbc/AjaxConnectionDS</res-ref-name>
  <res-type>javax.sql.DataSource</res-type>
  <res-auth>Container</res-auth>
</resource-ref>
```

Select **File>Save All** to save the Ajax project. The *C:\JDeveloper\mywork\AjaxApp\AjaxApp-data-sources.xml* file should have a managed data source configured with JNDI `jdbc/AjaxConnectionDS`. A managed-data-source element gets added to the data sources file by default when the JDBC connection is configured in Databases window. A managed data source may also be configured declaratively in the *AjaxApp-data-sources.xml* by adding the following connection pool and managed data source definitions to the *AjaxApp-data-sources.xml* file.

```
<connection-pool name="AjaxConnectionPool" validate-
connection="false"><connection-factory            factory-
class="oracle.jdbc.pool.OracleDataSource"   user="OE"
password="->jdbc:oracle:thin:@localhost:1521:ORCL_OE"
url="jdbc:oracle:thin:@localhost:1521:ORCL"/>
```

```
    </connection-pool><managed-data-source
name="AjaxDataSource"                  connection-pool-
name="AjaxConnectionPool"                        jndi-
name="jdbc/AjaxConnectionDS"   user="OE"   password="-
>AjaxConnectionPool_OE" tx-level="global"/>
```

2.3 Sending an Ajax Request

In this chapter, we shall create an Ajax web application that validates data input in a HTML form. Data added to the HTML form is sent asynchronously to the server. On the server side, a HTTP servlet processes the input from the form and returns a response as an XML DOM object. In the client application the response from the server is processed and a message is output about the validity of the data added. In the example application, an input form is used to create a catalog entry that is sent to the server and updated in the database in a server side Servlet. A developer would be interested in ascertaining if a catalog Id specified in the input form is not already taken in the catalog database. As the client specifies the catalog Id field, an XMLHttpRequest is sent to the server with each modification in the input field. A response from the server in the form of an XML DOM object provides information to the client about the validity of the catalog Id value specified. Without Ajax, the complete form would have to be posted to the server and the client JSP reloaded after a response is received from the server. The procedure to send an XMLHttpRequest request is as follows.

1. Create a XMLHttpRequest object.
2. Open a XMLHttpRequest request.
3. Register a callback method to be invoked when the request is complete.
4. Send a XMLHttpRequest request.
5. Process the XML response and set HTML page content.

An XMLHttpRequest request is initiated from an HTML form that has input fields for creating a catalog entry. The XMLHttpRequest is initiated from the Catalog Id field, which is required to be validated. A JavaScript function, validateCatalogId() is invoked with onkeyup event. To the *input.jsp* add an input form with the <form> element. The input form has an input field for creating a catalog entry in Oracle database table CATALOG. The Catalog Id field is for specifying the Catalog Id and is the field we need to validate.

```
<form    name="validationForm"    action="validateForm"
method="post">
  <table>
  <tr><td>Catalog Id:</td><td><input    type="text"
          size="20"
          id="catalogId"
          name="catalogId"
          onkeyup="validateCatalogId()"></td>
          <td><div id="validationMessage"></div></td>
  </tr>
  ….
  ….
  </table></form>
```

In the JavaScript file *input.js* create a JavaScript function
validateCatalogId() in which create a new XMLHttpRequest
object.

```
function validateCatalogId(){
var xmlHttpRequest=init();
  function init(){
  if (window.XMLHttpRequest) {
          return new XMLHttpRequest();
      } else if (window.ActiveXObject) {
      return new ActiveXObject("Microsoft.XMLHTTP");
      }
   }
}
```

Next, in the JavaScript file construct the URL to which the
XMLHttpRequest is to be sent. As the FormValidationServlet
is mapped to servlet URL validateForm, specify the URL as
validateForm with a catalogId parameter.

```
var catalogId=document.getElementById("catalogId");
xmlHttpRequest.open("GET", "validateForm?catalogId="+
encodeURIComponent(catalogId.value), true);
```

Register a callback event handler for the XMLHttpRequest using the
onreadystatechange property. In the example application, the
callback method is the processRequest function.

```
xmlHttpRequest.onreadystatechange=processRequest;
```

Send the XMLHttpRequest to the server using the send message. As
the HTTP method is GET, data sent with the send method is set to null.

```
xmlHttpRequest.send(null);
```

As the callback method is processRequest, the processRequest function is invoked when value of the readyState property changes. In the processRequest function, the readyState property value is retrieved to determine if request has loaded completely and if HTTP status is "OK".

```
function processRequest(){
if(xmlHttpRequest.readyState==4){
   if(xmlHttpRequest.status==200){
      processResponse();
   }
  }
}
```

2.4 Processing an Ajax Request on the Server Side

To the server an Ajax request is just like any other HTTP request. In this section, the server side processing of the XMLHttpRequest request sent to the server is discussed. The XMLHttpRequest is sent to url validateForm?catalogId=catalogId. Variable catalogId is the value of parameter catalogId. As the FormValidationServlet is mapped to url validateForm, the servlet gets invoked. As the XMLHttpRequest method is GET, the doGet method of the servlet gets invoked. In the doGet method, retrieve the value of the catalogId parameter.

```
String catalogId = request.getParameter("catalogId");
```

To obtain data from the database, create a JDBC connection from a datasource. Create a DataSource object using an InitialContext object lookup and from the DataSource object obtain a Connection object.

```
InitialContext initialContext = new InitialContext();
javax.sql.DataSource ds = (javax.sql.DataSource)
initialContext.lookup("java:comp/env/jdbc/AjaxConnect
ionDS");
java.sql.Connection conn = ds.getConnection();
```

Create a Statement object, specify a SQL query to retrieve data from the database for the catalogId value specified in the input form, and obtain a ResultSet object with the executeQuery(String query) method of the Statement object.

```
Statement stmt = conn.createStatement();
           String query = "SELECT * from OE.Catalog
WHERE catalogId=" + "'" +
           catalogId + "'";
ResultSet rs = stmt.executeQuery(query);
```

Set the content type of the `HttpServletResponse` to `text/xml`, and set the cache-control header to `no-cache`.

```
response.setContentType("text/xml");
response.setHeader("Cache-Control", "no-cache");
```

The response from the servlet is in the form of a XML DOM object. Construct an XML DOM object that contains information about the validity of the `catalogId` field value. If the `ResultSet` object is empty, the `catalogId` field value is not defined in the database table Catalog, therefore the `catalogId` field value is valid. If the `ResultSet` object has data, the `catalogId` value is already defined in the database, therefore, the `catalogId` field value is not valid. The business logic to define a valid Catalog Id may be customized. The Catalog Id input may be matched to a pattern using regular expressions API available in the `java.util.regex` package. We have used the business logic that if a catalog id is not defined in the database it is valid. If a catalog entry is already defined for the `catalogId` value include the field values of the different fields in the input form in the XML DOM object. The XML DOM object is required to have a root element. In the example application, the XML DOM object has a `<valid></valid>` element that specifies the validity of the Catalog Id field value.

```
if (rs.next()) {
out.println("<catalog>" + "<valid>false</valid>" +
"<journal>" +
rs.getString(2) + "</journal>" + "<publisher>" +
rs.getString(3) + "</publisher>" + "<edition>" +
rs.getString(4) + "</edition>" + "<title>" +
rs.getString(5) + "</title>" + "<author>" +
rs.getString(6) + "</author>" + "</catalog>");
} else {
out.println("<valid>true</valid>");
}
```

If the `catalogId` field value is not defined in the database, a catalog entry may be added for the `catalogId` value by obtaining a JDBC connection to the database, and adding a catalog entry with an SQL INSERT statement. Copy the `FormValidationServlet`, which is listed below, to FormValidationServlet.java file in the Ajax project.

```
package ajax;
import java.io.*;
import java.sql.*;
import javax.naming.InitialContext;
import javax.servlet.*;
import javax.servlet.http.*;

public     class     FormValidationServlet     extends
HttpServlet {
    public   void   doGet(HttpServletRequest   request,
HttpServletResponse response)
        throws ServletException, IOException {
        try {
            //Obtain value of Catalog Id field to ve
validated.
    String                catalogId                =
request.getParameter("catalogId");
            //Obtain Connection
    InitialContext        initialContext     =        new
InitialContext();
    javax.sql.DataSource  ds  =  (javax.sql.DataSource)
initialContext.lookup(
    "java:comp/env/jdbc/AjaxConnectionDS");
    java.sql.Connection conn = ds.getConnection();
            //Obtain result set
    Statement stmt = conn.createStatement();
    String query = "SELECT * from OE.Catalog WHERE
catalogId=" + "'" +catalogId + "'";
    ResultSet rs = stmt.executeQuery(query);
            //  set  headers  before  accessing  the
Writer
    response.setContentType("text/xml");
    response.setHeader("Cache-Control", "no-cache");
    PrintWriter out = response.getWriter();
            // then write the response
    //If result set is empty set valid element to
true
    if (rs.next()) {
        out.println("<catalog>"                     +
"<valid>false</valid>" + "<journal>" +
    rs.getString(2) + "</journal>" + "<publisher>"
+
        rs.getString(3) + "</publisher>" + "<edition>"
+
```

```
        rs.getString(4) + "</edition>" + "<title>" +
        rs.getString(5) + "</title>" + "<author>" +
        rs.getString(6) + "</author>" + "</catalog>");
    } else {
    out.println("<valid>true</valid>");
        }
      rs.close();
      stmt.close();
      conn.close();
        } catch (javax.naming.NamingException e) {
        } catch (SQLException e) {
        }
    }
    public  void  doPost(HttpServletRequest  request,
HttpServletResponse response)
        throws ServletException, IOException {
        try {
      //Obtain Connection
  InitialContext        initialContext        =        new
InitialContext();
    javax.sql.DataSource ds =
      (javax.sql.DataSource)
    initialContext.lookup("java:comp/env/jdbc/AjaxConn
    ectionDS");
    java.sql.Connection conn = ds.getConnection();
    String                catalogId                =
request.getParameter("catalogId");
    String journal = request.getParameter("journal");
    String                publisher                =
request.getParameter("publisher");
    String edition = request.getParameter("edition");
    String title = request.getParameter("title");
    String author = request.getParameter("author");
    Statement stmt = conn.createStatement();
    String sql = "INSERT INTO Catalog VALUES(" + "\'"
+ catalogId +
                "\'" + "," + "\'" + journal + "\'" +
"," + "\'" + publisher +
                "\'" + "," + "\'" + edition + "\'" +
"," + "\'" + title + "\'" +
                "," + "\'" + author + "\'" + ")";
    stmt.execute(sql);
    response.sendRedirect("catalog.jsp");

    stmt.close();
    conn.close();
        } catch (javax.naming.NamingException e) {
```

```
        response.sendRedirect("error.jsp");
    } catch (SQLException e) {
  response.sendRedirect("error.jsp");
        }
    }
}
```

2.5 Processing an Ajax Response

In this section the Ajax XML response is retrieved and the input web page updated to indicate the validity of the Catalog Id value and the input fields are autocompleted if the Catalog Id is not valid. If the readyState property value is 4, which corresponds to a completed XMLHttpRequest, and the status property value is 200, which corresponds to HTTP status "OK", the processResponse() function gets invoked. In the processResponse function, obtain the value for the responseXML property.

```
var xmlMessage=xmlHttpRequest.responseXML;
```

The responseXML object is an XML DOM object. Obtain the value of the <valid/> element using getElementsByTagName(String) method.

```
var
valid=xmlMessage.getElementsByTagName("valid")[0].fir
stChild.nodeValue;
```

If the <valid/> element value is true, set the HTML of a div element in the Catalog Id field row to "Catalog Id is Valid". Enable the submit button in the input form.

```
if(valid=="true"){
var
validationMessage=document.getElementById("validation
Message");
validationMessage.innerHTML = "Catalog Id is Valid";
document.getElementById("submitForm").disabled      =
false;
    }
```

If the <valid/> element value is false, set the HTML of the div element in Catalog ID field row to "Catalog Id is not Valid". Disable the submit button, and set the values of the other input fields.

```
if(valid=="false"){
var
validationMessage=document.getElementById("validation
Message");
validationMessage.innerHTML  =  "Catalog  Id  is  not
Valid";
document.getElementById("submitForm").disabled       =
true;
}
```

The *input.js* JavaScript file is listed below.

```
function validateCatalogId(){
  var xmlHttpRequest=init();
  function init(){
   if (window.XMLHttpRequest) {
        return new XMLHttpRequest();
      } else if (window.ActiveXObject) {
         return new
         ActiveXObject("Microsoft.XMLHTTP");
       }
    }
    var
    catalogId=document.getElementById("catalogId");
    xmlHttpRequest.open("GET",
    "validateForm?catalogId="+
    encodeURIComponent(catalogId.value), true);
    xmlHttpRequest.onreadystatechange=processRequest;
   xmlHttpRequest.send(null);
  function processRequest(){
    if(xmlHttpRequest.readyState==4){
       if(xmlHttpRequest.status==200){
        processResponse();
      }
   }
  }
}
function processResponse(){
  var xmlMessage=xmlHttpRequest.responseXML;
  var
  valid=xmlMessage.getElementsByTagName("valid")[0].
  firstChild.nodeValue;

if(valid=="true"){
 var
 validationMessage=document.getElementById("validatio
 nMessage");
 validationMessage.innerHTML = "Catalog Id is Valid";
```

```
document.getElementById("submitForm").disabled =
false;
var
journalElement=document.getElementById("journal");
journalElement.value = "";
var
publisherElement=document.getElementById("publisher"
);
publisherElement.value = "";
var
editionElement=document.getElementById("edition");
editionElement.value = "";
var titleElement=document.getElementById("title");
titleElement.value = "";
var authorElement=document.getElementById("author");
authorElement.value = "";
}
if(valid=="false"){
var
validationMessage=document.getElementById("validatio
nMessage");
validationMessage.innerHTML = "Catalog Id is not
Valid";
document.getElementById("submitForm").disabled =
true;
var
journal=xmlMessage.getElementsByTagName("journal")[0
].firstChild.nodeValue;
var
publisher=xmlMessage.getElementsByTagName("publisher
")[0].firstChild.nodeValue;
var
edition=xmlMessage.getElementsByTagName("edition")[0
].firstChild.nodeValue;
var
title=xmlMessage.getElementsByTagName("title")[0].fi
rstChild.nodeValue;
var
author=xmlMessage.getElementsByTagName("author")[0].
firstChild.nodeValue;
var
journalElement=document.getElementById("journal");
journalElement.value = journal;
var
publisherElement=document.getElementById("publisher"
);
publisherElement.value = publisher;
```

```
var
editionElement=document.getElementById("edition");
    editionElement.value = edition;
var titleElement=document.getElementById("title");
titleElement.value = title;
var authorElement=document.getElementById("author");
authorElement.value = author;
  }
 }
}
```

To the *input.jsp* add input fields for journal, publisher, edition, title, and author and also add a Submit button. The *input.jsp* is listed below.

```
<html>
<head>
</head>
<body>
<h1>Ajax Web Application</h1>
<form    name="validationForm"    action="validateForm"
method="post">
<table>
<tr><td>Catalog Id:</td><td><input    type="text"
        size="20"
          id="catalogId"
          name="catalogId"
      onkeyup="validateCatalogId()"></td>
        <td><div id="validationMessage"></div></td>
</tr>
<tr><td>Journal:</td><td><input    type="text"
        size="20"
          id="journal"
          name="journal"></td>
</tr>
<tr><td>Publisher:</td><td><input    type="text"
        size="20"
          id="publisher"
          name="publisher"></td>
</tr>
<tr><td>Edition:</td><td><input    type="text"
        size="20"
          id="edition"
          name="edition"></td>
</tr>
<tr><td>Title:</td><td><input    type="text"
        size="20"
            id="title"
```

```
                    name="title"></td>
</tr>
<tr><td>Author:</td><td><input        type="text"
            size="20"
             id="author"
            name="author"></td>
</tr>
<tr><td><input       type="submit"
            value="Create Catalog"
             id="submitForm"
            name="submitForm"></td>
</tr>
</table>
</form>
</body>
</html>
```

Next, include the JavaScript file *input.js* to the JSP file *input.jsp*. Position the cursor in the `<head></head>` element in *input.jsp* and drag and dropt *input.js* from the **Application Navigator**. A `<script/>` element gets added to *input.jsp*. Modify the `<script/>` element to add a `type` attribute.

```
<script language="JavaScript" type="text/javascript"
src="input.js"></script>
```

We also need to modify the *catalog.jsp*, which is the JSP that gets displayed if a catalog entry gets created. Add the following scritplet to *catalog.jsp*.

```
<%out.println("Catalog Entry Created"); %>
```

Similarly, to the *error.jsp* add scriptlet that outputs an error message.

```
<%out.println("Error in creating Catalog Entry"); %>
```

Select **File>Save** All to save all the Ajax application files. Next, we shall run the Ajax web application in JDeveloper 11g. Right-click on the input.jsp file in **Application Navigator**, and select **Run** as shown in Fig. 2.13.

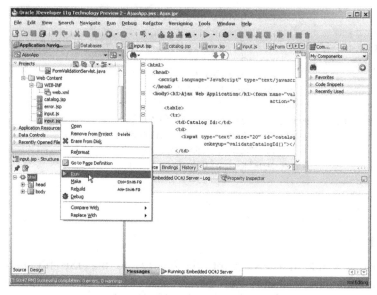

Fig. 2.13 Running Ajax Web Application

The input form gets displayed. Start adding data to Catalog Id field. An XMLHttpRequest gets sent to the server to verify the validity of the data being added. If the Catalog Id field value is valid, a "Catalog Id is Valid" message gets displayed as shown in Fig. 2.14.

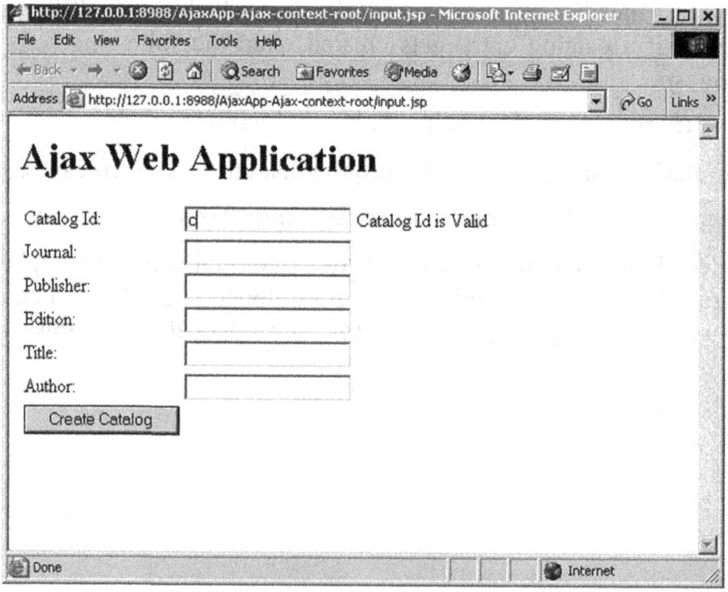

Fig. 2.14 Validating Catalog Id

An XMLHttpRequest request gets sent with each modification to the Catalog Id input field as shown in Fig. 2.15.

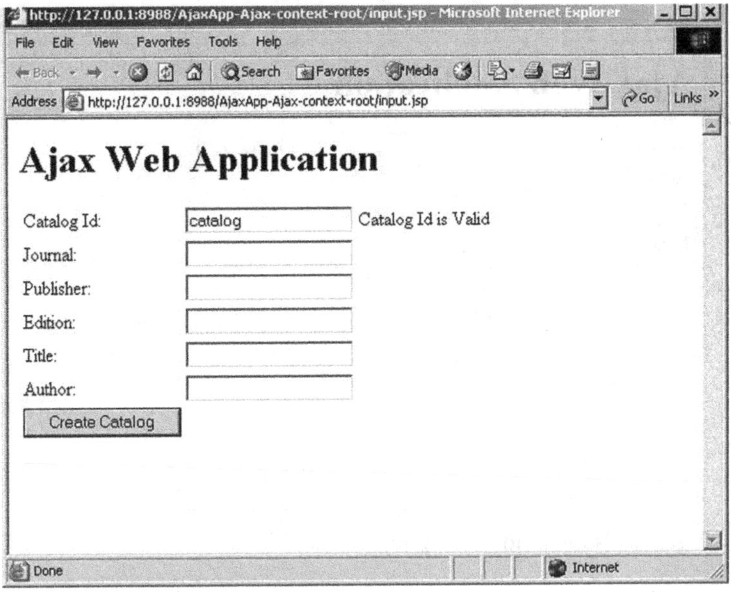

Fig. 2.15 Dynamic Validation

If a value is added that is already defined in the database, a "Catalog Id is not Valid" message gets displayed and the **Submit** button gets disabled as shown in Fig. 2.16.

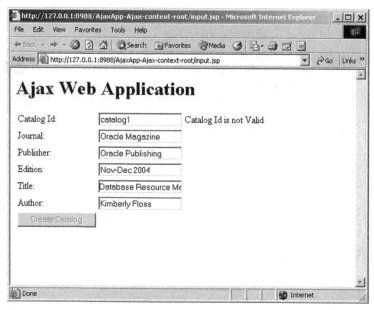

Fig. 2.16 Non-Valid Catalog Id

Specify a Catalog Id field value that is valid and click on **Create Catalog** button to add a catalog entry as shown in Fig. 2.17.

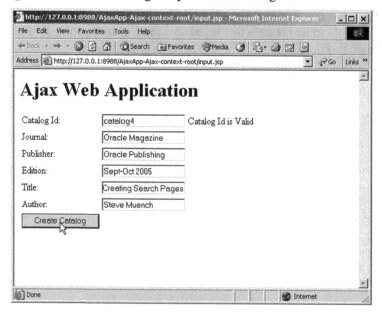

Fig. 2.17 Creating a Catalog Entry for a Valid Catalog Id

The form gets posted to the server with POST method, because the method specified in <form/> element is POST. A catalog entry for the specified field values gets added to the database. If subsequently, a Catalog Id value of Catalog4 is re-specified, an XMLHttpRequest gets sent to the server, and the response has <valid/> element set to false. The validation message gets displayed to indicate that the Catalog Id is not valid as shown in Fig. 2.18.

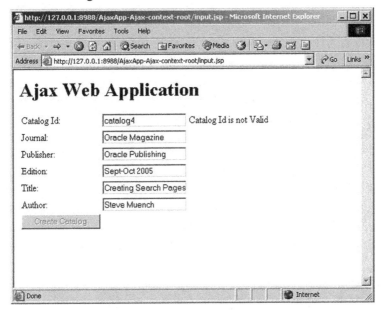

Fig. 2.18 A Catalog Id becomes non-valid after a catalog entry is created

2.5 Summary

The Ajax technique provides dynamic validation of data added to an input form using the XMLHttpRequest object. Ajax is a technique, therefore a combination other than JavaScript, DOM and Servlet may be used. For example, the server side application may be a PHP script instead of a servlet. In this chapter we used Ajax to validate an input form in JDeveloper 11g. HTTP Servlet is used on the server side.

3 Less JavaScript with Prototype

3.1 Introduction

In the previous chapter we discussed the procedure to create an Ajax web application. The reader might have noticed that the client script included a lot of JavaScript. Prototype is a JavaScript library for developing dynamic web applications. The objective of the prototype library is to reduce the JavaScript code with prototype functions and to provide Ajax functionality with `Ajax.Request` and `Ajax.Updater` classes. In a previous chapter we developed an Ajax application to validate an input form. The same application could be developed with the Prototype library, as we shall discuss in this chapter.

3.2 Overview of Prototype

The Prototype library provides various utility functions to reduce JavaScript code, and provides Ajax classes to send an `XMLHttpRequest` request. Prototype also provides functions for DOM processing, form processing, and event processing. We shall discuss the main Prototype functions and classes next.

3.2.1 $() function

The `$()` function is used to replace the `document.getElementById()` function. For example a non-prototype JavaScript retrieves a form element `formDiv` as follows.

```
var formDiv =document.getElementById("formDiv");
```

The `formDiv` element may be retrieved with prototype as follows.

```
var formDiv =$('formDiv');
```

3.2.2 $F() function

The $F() function is used to retrieve the value of a form element. For example, a non-prototype JavaScript obtains a form field value as follows.

```
var field1=document.getElementById("field1").value;
```

The $F() function reduces the code to retrieve the form filed value as shown below.

```
var field1=$F('field1');
```

3.2.3 $A() function

The $A() function is used to create an Array object from a node list or an enumerable list. For example, an Array object may be created from a node list object and the Array object navigated to retrieve node values. In the following listing the HTML value of the first journal node in an XML document is retrieved with the $A() function.

```
var nodeList=xmlMessage.getElementsByTagName
("journal");
var journalValue=$A(nodeList).first().innerHTML;
```

3.2.4 $H() function

The $H() function converts enumerations into enumerable Hash objects. For example, variable journal is an enumeration of journals.

```
var  journal={first: Oracle Magazine,  second: ONJava,
third: AJAX Magazine};
```

The enumeration may be transformed into a hash with the $H() function.

```
var journals=$H(journal);
```

3.2.5 $R() function

The $R() function is used to represent an ObjectRange object. For example, the following ObjectRange object may be represented with the $H() function.

```
ObjectRange range=new ObjectRange(10, 25, false);
```

The corresponding $R() function representation is as follows.

```
var range=$R(10, 25, false);
```

3.2.6 $w() Function

The $w() function creates an array from a string using the whitepaces in the string as delimiters. For example, the following Array, catalogIds, may be created from a string that consists of Catalog Ids delimited by whitespace using the $w() function.

```
var catalogIds=$w("catalog1 catalog2 catalog3");
```

The catalogIds array may be represented as follows.

```
['catalog1', 'catalog2', 'catalog3']
```

3.2.7 Try.these function()

The Try.these() function tries a sequence of functions until one of the function runs.   For   example,   different   browsers   create   an XMLHttpRequest differently. Try.these() function may be used to create an XMLHttpRequest object as shown in following listing.

```
function getXMLHttpRequest(){
return Try.these(
   function() {return new XMLHttpRequest();},
   function() {
      return new ActiveXObject("Microsoft.XMLHTTP");}
);}
```

3.2.8 Ajax.Request Class

The Prototype library provides the Ajax.Request class to send an XMLHttpRequest request. The The Ajax.Request constructor may be used to create an Ajax.Request object.

```
Ajax.Request                                 ajaxRequest=new
Ajax.Request(url,options);
```

The options value may be specified with a JavaScript Object Notation (JSON). For example, an Ajax.Request object may be created that sends an XMLHttpRequest to a servlet url, which includes a userid parameter.

```
var userid=$F('userid');
var url = 'servletURL';
var pars = 'userid=' + userid;
var myAjax = new Ajax.Request(
url, {method: 'get',
parameters: pars, onComplete: showResponse});
```

The `url` specifies the servlet url to which the request is sent. The `options` are specified as a JSON; the `method` property specifies that the request be sent using HTTP `GET` method; the default method is `POST`. The `method` value (`get/post`) is required to be specified in lowercase. The `parameters` property specifies the parameters to be sent with the url. The `onComplete` property specifies the function to be invoked when the request is complete. Similarly, `onLoading`, `onLoaded`, and `onInteractive` property functions may be specified. The `onLoading` property represents the state when an `XMLHttpRequest` has been initiated, but the request has not yet been sent. The `onLoaded` property represents the state when the request has been sent, but a response has not yet been received. The `onInteractive` property represents the state when the some of the response has been received. The `onComplete` property represents the state when all of the response has been recieved. The `onComplete` property function, or a property function representing some other state of the request, is invoked by an argument containing the `XMLHttpRequest` object and another argument containing the response HTTP header. Some of the commonly used `Ajax.Request` options are discussed in Table 3.1.

Table 3.1 AjaxRequest Options

Property	Description
method	Specifies method of HTTP request. Default value is 'post'. Type is string.
parameters	List of parameters that are sent with the HTTP request. Type is string.
asynchronous	Specifies if the XMLHttpRequest be sent asynchronously. Default is true.
postBody	If HTTP request method is 'post', specifies the request's body.
requestHeaders	Specifies an array of HTTP headers to be sent with the request.
onLoading, onLoaded, onInteractive, onComplete	Specifies the functions that are invoked at various stages of the request. Recieves an argument representing the XMLHttpRequest and an argument representing the response header.

Table 3.1 (continued)

Property	Description
onSuccess, onFailure, onException	Specifies the function to be invoked when AJAX request completes successfully, or fails, or generates an exception. Similar to onComplete function, the function recieves an argument representing the XMLHttpRequest and an argument representing the response header.

3.2.9 Ajax.Updater Class

`Ajax.Updater` class is a sub class of `Ajax.Request` class and is used to update a specified DOM element with an `XMLHttpRequest` response. The `Ajax.Updater` constructor may be used to create an `Ajax.Updater` object as shown below.

```
var  ajaxRequest=new  Ajax.Updater(container,  url,
options);
```

The `container` parameter may be an element id, an element object, or an object with two properties; `object.success` and `object.failure`. The `object.success` element is used for updating if the Ajax call succeeds and the `object.failure` element is used if the Ajax call fails. The `url` parameter specifies the `url` to which the request is sent. The `options` parameter specifies the Ajax options, which are the same as for `Ajax.Request` class. In addition to the `Ajax.Request` options, an insertion class may be specified with `insertion` property. Insertion class value may be `Insertion.Before` (adds HTML before the element), `Insertion.After`(adds HTML after the element), `Insertion.Top`(adds HTML as a first child of the element), or `Insertion.Bottom`(adds HTML as the last child of the element). Another option that may be specified with `Ajax.Updater` is `evalScripts`, which indicates if scripts shall be evaluated when the response is received. Default value of `evalScripts` is `false`. For example, send an `XMLHttpRequest` with `Ajax.Updater` to update a form element, `userid`, with the response HTML.

```
var ajaxRequest = new Ajax.Updater('userid', url,
{method: 'get',
 parameters: pars});
```

3.2.10 Ajax.PeriodicalUpdater Class

The `Ajax.PeriodicalUpdater` class is similar to `Ajax.Updater` class and is used to update a form element periodically. The frequency with which the element is updated is specified with the `frequency` option. The constructor for `Ajax.PeriodicalUpdater` is the same as `Ajax.Updater`. For example, update a `validationMessage` div periodically.

```
Var ajaxRequest= new Ajax.PeriodicalUpdater
('validationMessage', url,
   {frequency: '2',
   method: 'get',
   parameters: pars
   });
```

3.3 Installing Prototype

We shall be using the same application that we developed in the previous chapter and add prototype functionality to the user interface. Download the latest version of prototype libray[1]. Copy *prototype.js* to the *public_html* directory of the Ajax project in JDeveloper 11g. The *prototype.js* file should be in the same directory as the *input.jsp* as shown in Fig. 3.1.

---

[1] Prototype Library- http://www.prototypejs.org/

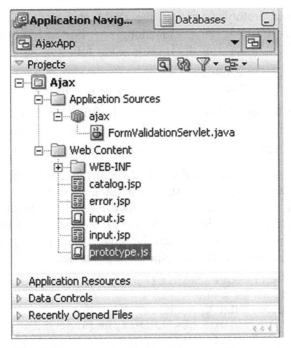

Fig. 3.1 Prototype Application Directory Structure

3.4 Configuring Prototype in AJAX Web Application

In this section we shall add prototype library functions and classes to the Ajax application *input.jsp*. To access the *prototype.js* library add the following <script/> element to *input.jsp*.

```
<script src="prototype.js" type="text/javascript">
</script>
```

In the Ajax application version without the prototype library, the catalogId field is retrieved with get getElementById() function and the value is retrieved with value attribute.

```
var
catalogId=document.getElementById("catalogId").value;
```

Retrieve the catalogId value with prototype function $F().

```
var catalogId=$F('catalogId');
```

In the non-prototype version, the DOM elements are retrieved with `getElementById()` function. For example the `validationMessage` div is retrieved as follows.

```
var validationMessage=
document.getElementById("validationMessage");
```

Replace the `getElementById()` function with prototype function `$()`.

```
var validationMessage=$('validationMessage');
```

In the non-prototype version an `XMLHttpRequest` object is created with the `XMLHttpRequest` constructor or the `ActiveXObject` constructor. The callback method is registered with the `XMLHttpRequest` object and the HTTP request sent to the server. The callback method is invoked when the request state changes and when the request is complete the HTTP response is processed.

```
var xmlHttpRequest=init();
  function init(){
if (window.XMLHttpRequest) {
        return new XMLHttpRequest();
      } else if (window.ActiveXObject) {
        return                            new
ActiveXObject("Microsoft.XMLHTTP");
      }
}
xmlHttpRequest.onreadystatechange=processRequest;
xmlHttpRequest.send(null);

function processRequest(){

if(xmlHttpRequest.readyState==4){
   if(xmlHttpRequest.status==200){
     processResponse();
   }
  }
}
```

The prototype library provides `Ajax.Request` class to send an `XMLHttpRequest` request. Define a variable for servlet url and a variable for url parameters.

```
var catalogId=$F('catalogId');
var url = 'validateForm';
var pars ='catalogId='+catalogId;
```

Create an `Ajax.Request` object with the servlet url. Set the options property `method` to 'get'. Specify the `parameters` options property and set the `asynchronous` property to `true`. Specify the callback method with the `onComplete` property. The `XMLHttpRequest` gets created and sent to the specified url. When the request is complete, the `showResponse` function gets invoked. The function registered with the `onComplete` property gets invoked with an argument containing the `XMLHttpRequest` object and an argument containing the HTTP response header.

```
var ajaxRequest = new Ajax.Request(
    url,
    {
      method: 'get',
      parameters: pars,
      asynchronous: true,
    onComplete: showResponse
    });
}
function showResponse(xmlHttpRequest, responseHeader)
{//Process Http response and update input form
        }
```

The `showResponse` function retrieves the XML response from the server and updates the input form.

```
var xmlMessage = xmlHttpRequest.responseXML;
```

The *input.js* with JavaScript code replaced with prototype library functions and `Ajax.Request` class is listed below.

```
function validateCatalogId(){
var catalogId=$F('catalogId');
var url = 'validateForm';
var pars ='catalogId='+catalogId;
var ajaxRequest = new Ajax.Request(
    url,
    {
      method: 'get',
      parameters: pars,
      asynchronous: true,
      onComplete: showResponse
    });
}
function showResponse(xmlHttpRequest, responseHeader)
{
var xmlMessage = xmlHttpRequest.responseXML;
```

```
var
valid=xmlMessage.getElementsByTagName("valid")[0].fir
stChild.nodeValue;
if(valid=="true"){
var validationMessage=$('validationMessage');
validationMessage.innerHTML = "Catalog Id is Valid";
$('submitForm').disabled = false;
var journalElement=$('journal');
journalElement.value = "";
var publisherElement=$('publisher');
publisherElement.value = "";
var editionElement=$('edition');
editionElement.value = "";
var titleElement=$('title');
titleElement.value = "";
var authorElement=$('author');
authorElement.value = "";
}
if(valid=="false"){
var validationMessage=$('validationMessage');
validationMessage.innerHTML = "Catalog  Id  is  not
Valid";
$('submitForm').disabled = true;
var
journal=xmlMessage.getElementsByTagName("journal")[0]
.firstChild.nodeValue;
var
publisher=xmlMessage.getElementsByTagName("publisher"
)[0].firstChild.nodeValue;
var
edition=xmlMessage.getElementsByTagName("edition")[0]
.firstChild.nodeValue;
var
title=xmlMessage.getElementsByTagName("title")[0].fir
stChild.nodeValue;
var
author=xmlMessage.getElementsByTagName("author")[0].f
irstChild.nodeValue;
var journalElement=$('journal');
journalElement.value = journal;
var publisherElement=$('publisher');
publisherElement.value = publisher;
var editionElement=$('edition');
editionElement.value = edition;
var titleElement=$('title');
titleElement.value = title;
```

```
var authorElement=$('author');
authorElement.value = author;
   }
}
```

Replace the *input.js* in the Ajax web application with the *input.js* with the Prototype functions and classes. Run the *input.jsp* in JDeveloper 11g to generate the same output as the non-prototype version of the Ajax application. Right-click on *input.jsp* and select **Run** as shown in Fig. 3.2.

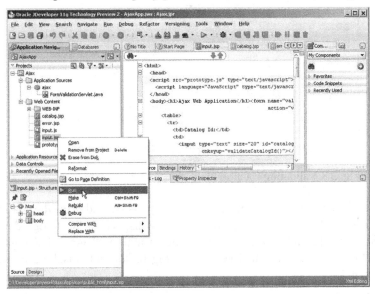

Fig. 3.2 Running Ajax Prototype Application

The catalog entry form gets displayed .Specify a catalog Id. An HTTP request gets sent to the server with the XMLHttpRequest object. Instructions about the validity of the Catalog Id get sent back to the browser, all without posting the web page to the server. A message gets displayed about the validity of the Catalog Id. For example, if a Catalog Id value is specified that is not already in the database message "Catalog Id is Valid" gets displayed as shown in Fig. 3.3.

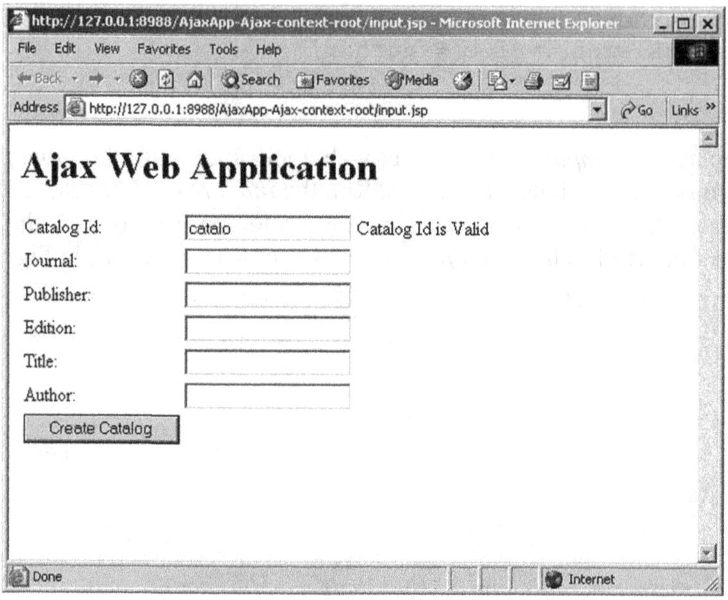

Fig. 3.3 Validating Catalog Id

Next, specify a Catalog Id value that is already in the database, catalog1 for example. A message gets displayed, "Catalog Id is not Valid". The form fields for the specified Catalog Id get filled with data from the database and the **Create Catalog** button gets disabled as shown in Fig. 3.4.

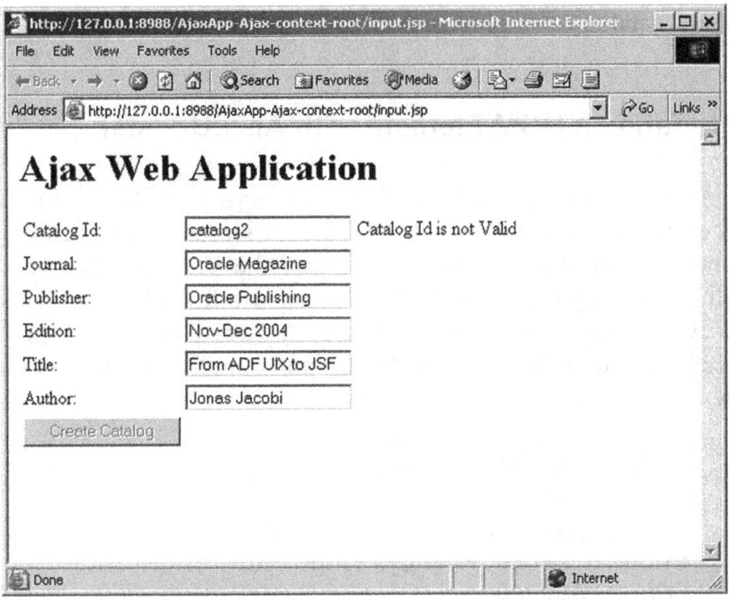

Fig. 3.4 Non Valid Catalog Id

To add a catalog entry, specify a Catalog Id that is not already in the database , specify the field values and click on **Create Catalog** button as shown in Fig. 3.5.

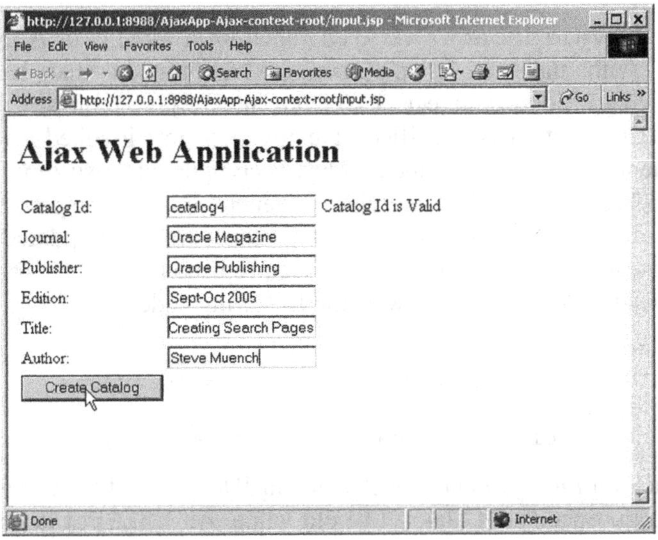

Fig. 3.5 Creating a Catalog Entry

A new catalog entry gets created.

3.5 Updating a DOM Element with Ajax.Updater

The prototype library provides another class, `Ajax.Updater` to update a DOM element's contents with the HTML from an XMLHttpRequest response. As an example we shall update the `validationMessage` element in the input form with HTML response from the server using the `Ajax.Updater` class. Create an `Ajax.Updater` object and specify the DOM element to update, the servlet url, and options parameters as shown below.

```
function validateCatalogId(){
var catalogId=$F('catalogId');
var url = 'validateForm';
var pars ='catalogId='+catalogId;
var ajaxRequest = new Ajax.Updater
('validationMessage',
     url,
     {
       method: 'get',
       parameters: pars
     });
}
```

Replace the `validateCatalogId` function in *input.js* in Ajax web application with the `validateCatalogId` function that has the `Ajax.Updater` class object to send the Ajax request. If an `onComplete` function is specified the function gets invoked after the DOM element specified to be updated has been updated. Also modify the `FormValidationServlet` servlet to generate a text response with which the `validationMessage` div's contents are to be updated with. In the `FormValidationServlet` servlet, replace the `if-else` block that generates the Ajax response with the following code.

```
if (rs.next()) {
   out.println("Catalog Id is not Valid");
      } else {
         out.println("Catalog Id is Valid");}
```

Right-click on *input.jsp* and select **Run** in JDeveloper 11g to produce the input form. Specify a Catalog Id field value. An XMLHttpRequest gets sent to the server and the `validationMessage` div gets updated with the response HTML as shown in Fig. 3.6.

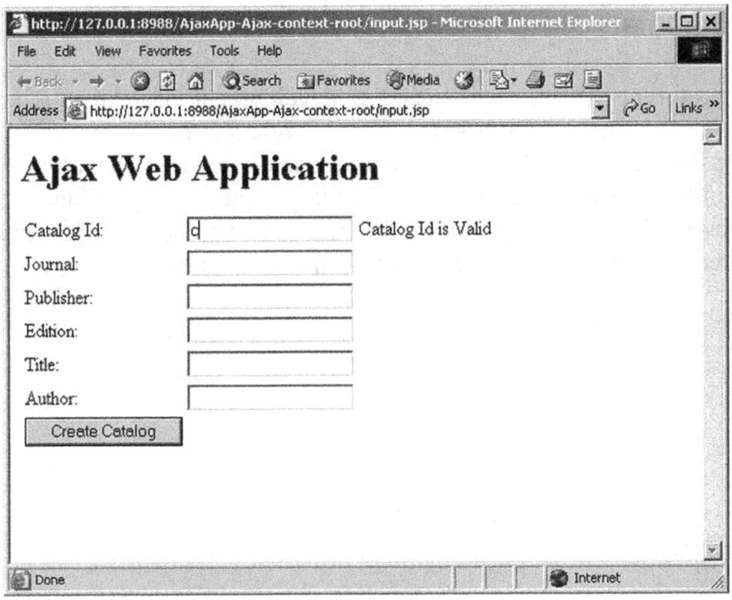

Fig. 3.6 Updating ValidationMessage Div

If a Catalog Id field value is specified that is not valid, the validationMessage div message gets updated to indicate that the Catalog Id value is not valid, as shown in Fig. 3.7.

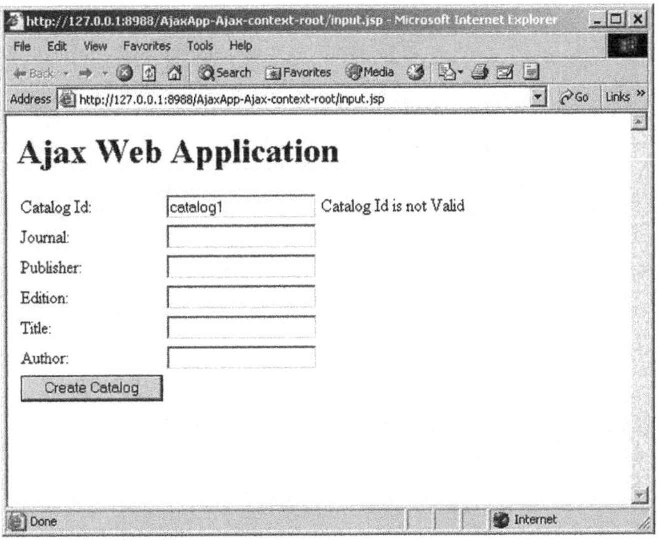

Fig. 3.7 Non Valid Catalog Id

3.6 Summary

The prototype library facilitates the development of Ajax applications with   `Ajax.Request,`   `Ajax.Updater`   and `Ajax.PeriodicalUpdater` classes, and   reduces   JavaScript code with utility functions. In this chapter we   added   prototype functions and classes to the Ajax web application that we developed in the previous chapter to reduce the JavaScript code in the web application.

4 Ajax with Java-GWT

4.1 Introduction

Google Web Toolkit (GWT) is a Java framework for developing Ajax applications. Ajax being a JavaScript based web technique, GWT generates the required JavaScript and HTML from the Java classes. GWT provides a library of dynamic, reusable user interface (UI) components for UI applications. Only a front-end Java class is required to be specified to create a GWT application. GWT applications may be run with commonly used browsers such as IE and Netscape and Safari.

4.2 Installing GWT

First, we need to download GWT 1.4[1]. Extract the zip file to a directory. Install a recent version of JDK if not already installed. We shall be using JDK 5.0. GWT does not require any installer application. All the required files are available in the directory in which the zip file is extracted.

GWT provides the command-line tool `applicationCreator` to generate a GWT application. GWT also provides a `projectCreator` tool to generate an Eclipse project for the GWT application, but we shall only discuss the command-line GWT application.

A GWT application may be run in two modes: `hosted` mode and `web` mode. In hosted mode a GWT application is run as Java bytecode in the JVM. In web mode the GWT application is run as JavaScript and HTML created with Java-to-JavaScript compiler.

GWT has four main components.

1. GWT Java-to-JavaScript compiler. The Java-to-JavaScript compiler compiles a Java class into JavaScript and HTML. Java-to-JavaScript compiler is used to run a GWT application in web mode.

---

[1] Download GWT- http://code.google.com/webtoolkit/download.html

2. GWT Hosted Web Browser. The Hosted Web Browser is used to run a GWT application in hosted mode.
3. JRE Emulation Library. The JRE emulation library contains JavaScript implementations of the most commonly used Java standard class libraries.
4. GWT Web UI Class Library. The Web UI class library consists of classes and interfaces to create User Interface (UI) components (widgets) such as buttons and text fields.

4.3 Creating a GWT Application

The procedure to develop a GWT application is as follows.

1. Create a GWT application with the `applicationCreator` tool.
2. Modify the Java class to add UI components or other Java code.
3. Compile the Java class to JavaScript and HTML with GWT's Java-toJavaScript compiler.
4. Run the GWT application.

The syntax of the `applicationCreator` command is as follows.

```
applicationCreator [-eclipse projectName] [-out dir]
[-overwrite] [-ignore] className
```

-eclipse specifies the Eclipse IDE project for the GWT application.
-out specifies the directory in which output files are generated. The default is the current directory.
-overwrite specifies if existing files should be overwritten.
-ignore specifies that any existing files should be ignored, not overwritten.
-className specifies the front-end Java class for the GWT application.

The `applicationCreator` tool requires the final package of the class from which a GWT application is created to be "client". Create an example GWT application with the following command.

```
C:/GWT/gwt-windows-1.4.60>applicationCreator
com.gwt.client.CatalogForm
```

A   GWT   application   gets   created.   The   output   from   the `applicationCreator` command is shown in Fig. 4.1.

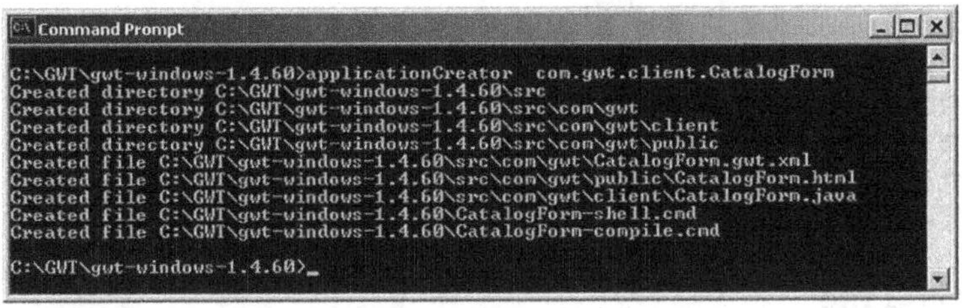

Fig. 4.1 Creating a GWT Application

The directory structure of the GWT application consists of `com/gwt` package, which is the project root package, in the `src` directory. Client-side source file/s, such as `com.gwt.client.CatalogForm.java`, and sub-packages are in the `com/gwt/client` package. Static resources, `CatalogForm.html`, are in the `com/gwt/public` package. `CatalogForm.html` is the wrapper HTML for the `CatalogForm` application and consists of a table with two `<td/>` cell elements. `CatalogForm.html` is listed below.

```
<html>
<head>
<title>Wrapper HTML for CatalogForm</title>
<style>
        body,td,a,div,.p{font-family:arial,sans-
        serif}
    div,td{color:#000000}
    a:link,.w,.w a:link{color:#0000cc}
    a:visited{color:#551a8b}
    a:active{color:#ff0000}
</style>
<!-- The module reference below is the link    -->
<!-- between html and your Web Toolkit module   -->
<meta name='gwt:module'
content='com.gwt.CatalogForm'>
</head>
    <!-- The body can have arbitrary html, or      -->
    <!-- you can leave the body empty if you want  -->
    <!-- to create a completely dynamic ui         -->
<body>
<!-- This script is required bootstrap stuff.   -->
<!-- You can put it in the HEAD, but startup    -->
<!-- is slightly faster if you include it here. -->
<script language="javascript" src="gwt.js"></script>
<!-- OPTIONAL: include this if you want history
support -->
```

```
<iframe id="__gwt_historyFrame"
style="width:0;height:0;border:0"></iframe>
<h1>CatalogForm</h1>
<p>
This is an example of a host page for the
CatalogForm application.
You can attach a Web Toolkit module to any HTML page
you like,
making it easy to add bits of AJAX functionality to
existing pages
without starting from scratch.
</p>
<table align=center>
<tr>
<td id="slot1"></td><td id="slot2"></td>
</tr>
</table>
</body>
</html>
```

A base module `CatalogForm.gwt.xml` gets created in the `com/gwt` directory. A module is a GWT configuration XML file. The base module inherits from the `com.google.gwt.user.User` module and is listed below.

```
<module>
<!--Inherit the core Web Toolkit stuff. -->
<inherits name='com.google.gwt.user.User'/>
<!--Specify the app entry point class. -->
<entry-point class='com.gwt.client.CatalogForm'/>
</module>
```

A module contains configuration information about inherited modules, entry-point class name, source path, and public path. When a module is loaded every entry-point class gets instantiated and its `EntryPoint.onModuleLoad()` method gets invoked. Source path specifies files in which packages/sub-packages are to be compiled into JavaScript. Public path specifies the directory path for static resources. In the preceding example, the entry point class is `com.gwt.client.CatalogForm`.

The `com.gwt.client.CatalogForm.java` class consists of a method `onModuleLoad()`. In the `onModuleLoad()` method a new `Button` and a `Label` are created. A `ClickListener` is added to the button. When the button is clicked the label text gets set to "Hello World" if the initial text is "". The button and the label are added to the `RootPanels` associated with the host HTML page table cell elements. A

RootPanel is a panel to which all other widgets are added. The Widget class is the root class for most of the user interface (UI) components. CatalogForm.java is listed below.

```java
package com.gwt.client;

import com.google.gwt.core.client.EntryPoint;
import com.google.gwt.user.client.ui.Button;
import com.google.gwt.user.client.ui.ClickListener;
import com.google.gwt.user.client.ui.Label;
import com.google.gwt.user.client.ui.RootPanel;
import com.google.gwt.user.client.ui.Widget;

/**
 * Entry point classes define
<code>onModuleLoad()</code>.
 */
public class CatalogForm implements EntryPoint {
  /**
   * This is the entry point method.
   */
  public void onModuleLoad() {
    final Button button = new Button("Click me");
    final Label label = new Label();
    button.addClickListener(new ClickListener() {
      public void onClick(Widget sender) {
        if (label.getText().equals(""))
          label.setText("Hello World!");
        else
          label.setText("");
      }
    });
// Assume that the host HTML has elements defined whose
    // IDs are "slot1", "slot2".  In a real app, you probably would not want
    // to hard-code IDs.  Instead, you could, for example, search for all
    // elements with a particular CSS class and replace them with widgets.
    //
    RootPanel.get("slot1").add(button);
    RootPanel.get("slot2").add(label);
  }
}
```

A hosted mode launch script, CatalogForm-shell, and a compilation script, CatalogForm-compile, also get created. Next, we shall run the GWT application in hosted mode and in web mode in JDeveloper 11g. First we shall run the GWT application in hosted mode. We need to create an application and a web project in JDeveloper. Select **File>New** and in the **New Gallery** window select **General** in **Categories** and **Application** in **Items** and click on **OK**. In the **Create Application** window specify an **Application Name** and click on **OK**. In the **Create Project** window click on **Cancel** as we shall be adding a Web Project to the application. An application gets added to **Application Navigator**. Select **File>New** and in the **New Gallery** window select **General>Projects** in **Categories** and **Web Project** in **Items** and click on **OK**. In the **Create Web Project Wizard** click on **Next**. Specify a **Project Name**, GWT, and specify Directory as C:/GWT/gwt-windows-1.4.60, which is the GWT installation directory, and click on **Next** as shown in Fig. 4.2.

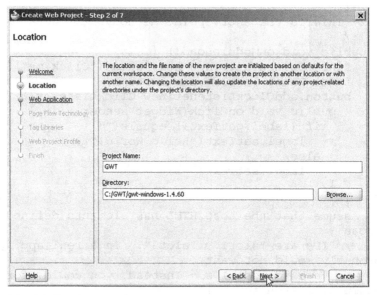

Fig. 4.2 Creating a Web Project

Select **J2EE 1.4** as the **Web Application Version** and click on **Next**. Click on **Next** in the **Page Flow Technology** window. In the **Tag Libraries** window click on **Next**. Specify **Document Root** as C:/GWT/gwt-windows-1.4.60/www and click on **Next** as shown in Fig. 4.3.

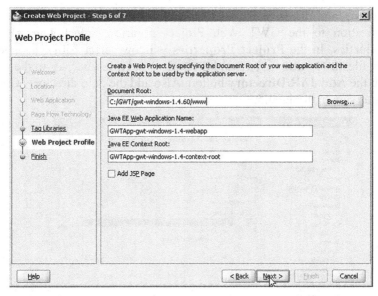

Fig. 4.3 Specifying Document Root

Click on **Finish**. The GWT Web Project gets created as shown in Fig. 4.4. The GWT application that we created with the `applicationCreator` gets added to the **Application Navigator**.

Fig. 4.4 GWT Application in JDeveloper

Next, add the GWT JAR files and Src directory of the GWT application to the GWT Web Project libraries. Select **Tools>Project Properties**. In the **Project Properties** window select **Libraries** and add JAR files GWT-user.jar and GWT-dev-windows.jar to the project with the **Add JAR/Directory** button. Also add the Src directory. Click on **OK** as shown in Fig. 4.5.

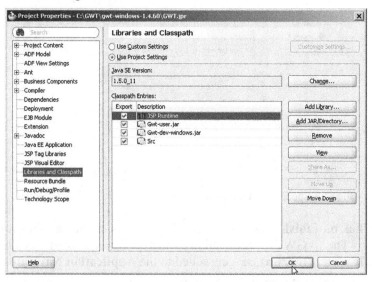

Fig. 4.5 GWT Libraries

Next, we shall configure the runtime settings for the GWT application for the hosted mode. Select **Tools>Project Properties**. In the **Project Properties** window select **Run/Debug/Profile** and select the **Default Run Configuration** and click on **Edit** as shown in Fig. 4.6.

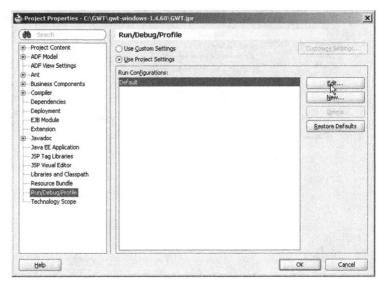

Fig. 4.6 Configuring Default Run Configuration

In the **Edit Run Configuration** window select the **Launch Settings** node and specify the **Default Run Target**, the **Program Arguments**, and the **Run Directory**. To run the GWT application in hosted mode, in the **Default Run Target** field select the GWTShell.class in the *gwt-dev-windows.jar*. In the **Program Arguments** field specify the following arguments.

```
-out C:/GWT/gwt-windows-1.4.60/www
com.gwt.CatalogForm/CatalogForm.html
```

In the **Run Directory** window specify the GWT installation directory, in which the GWT application was created. Click on **OK** as shown in Fig. 4.7.

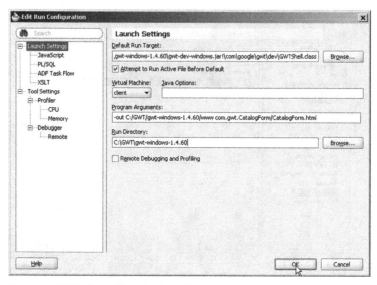

Fig. 4.7 GWT Hosted Mode Run Configuration

Click on **OK** in the **Project Properties** window. Next, we shall run the GWT application in hosted mode. Right-click on the GWT web project and select **Run** as shown in Fig. 4.8.

Fig. 4.8 Running GWT Application in Hosted Mode

The Tomcat servlet container gets started on port 8888. The *CatalogForm.java* application runs and button and a label UI components get added to the host HTML page. Click on the **Click me** button as shown in Fig. 4.9.

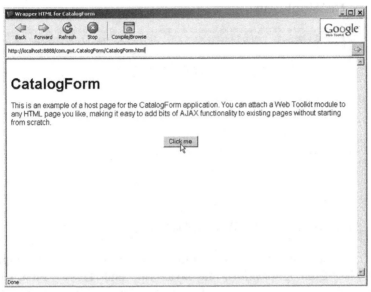

Fig. 4.9 GWT Application in Hosted Mode

"Hello World" text gets displayed in the host HTML page as shown in Fig. 4.10.

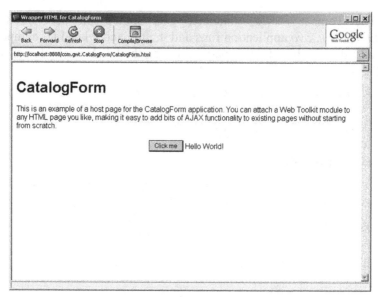

Fig. 4.10 Testing the GWT Application

To run the same GWT application in web mode we shall compile the Java class *CatalogForm.java* into JavaScript and HTML . First, we need to modify the runtime settings for the web mode. Select **Tools>Project Properties** and in the **Project Properties** window select **Run/Debug/Profile** and select the **Default Run Configuration**. Click on **Edit** and in the **Edit Run Configuration** window specify **Default Target** as the GWTCompiler.class and in the **Program Arguments** field specify the following arguments.

```
-out C:/GWT/gwt-windows-1.4.60/www
com.gwt.CatalogForm
```

The **Run Directory** is the same as for the hosted mode as shown in Fig. 4.11. Click on **OK** in the **Edit Run Configuration** window and the **Project Properties** window.

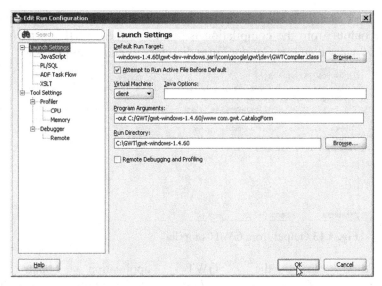

Fig. 4.11 Web Mode Run Configuration

Next, we shall run the GWT application in web mode. Right-click on the GWT web project and select **Run** as shown in Fig. 4.12.

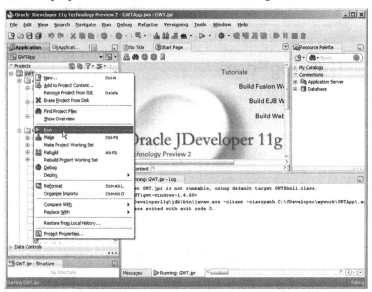

Fig. 4.12 Running GWT Application in Web Mode

The *CatalogForm.java* class gets compiled into HTML and JavaScript. The output from the compilation is copied to the *C:\GWT\gwt-windows-1.4.60\www\com.gwt.CatalogForm* directory as shown in Fig. 4.13.

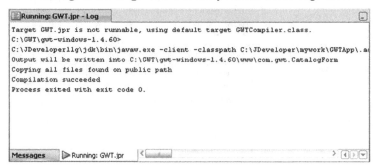

Fig. 4.13 Output from GWTCompiler

To   run   the   GWT   application   open   the *www/com.gwt.CatalogForm/CatalogForm.html* in a browser. The output is the same as for the hosted mode as shown in Fig. 4.14.

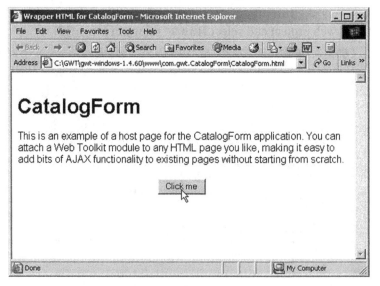

Fig. 4.14 GWT Application in Web Mode

Click on the button and a "Hello World" message gets displayed, same as for the hosted mode as shown in Fig. 4.15.

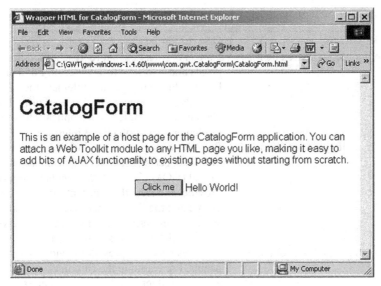

Fig. 4.15 Testing GWT Application in Web Mode

4.4 GWT Class Libraries

GWT provides various class packages for user interface classes and utility classes. GWT applications consist of widgets contained in panels. Widgets are user interface components such as buttons and labels. Panels such as DockPanel and HorizontalPanel are containers that layout the user interface components. Styles are applied to the widgets using CSS stylesheets. Some of the commonly used GWT packages are discussed in Table 4.1.

Table 4.1 GWT Packages

Package	Description
com.google.gwt.core.client	Core GWT classes that represent module entry points and interface to JavaScript. For a class to be a module entry point implement the EntryPoint interface. The CatalogForm.java class in the example GWT application implements the EntryPoint interface.
com.google.gwt.user.client	Provides classes representing a browser window (Window class), browser's Document Object Model (DOM class), DOM events (Event class). Provides the EventListener interface for browser events and the WindowCloseListener and WindowResizeListener interfaces to receive window closing and resizing events.
com.google.gwt.user.client.ui	Provides classes representing widgets and panels. For example the Button class represents a button widget and the TextArea class represents a text area widget. Most of the user interface classes extend the Widget class. Panels layout the widgets. For example, the HorizontalPanel lays out the widgets horizontally, the VerticalPanel lays out the widgets vertically, and the DockPanel lays out the widgets docked at the edges with the last widget taking up the center space. The FlowPanel lays out widgets in the HTML layout pattern and the FormPanel lays out HTML forms. Also provides interfaces to handle events generated by the widgets. For example, the ClickListener is registered with widgets generating a click event such as a button. The FormHandler interface handles form submit events.
com.google.gwt.xml.client	Provides classes and interfaces for generating and parsing XML documents. The XMLParser class is used to create and parse an XML document. The Document interface represents a document node and Element interface represents an element node.

4.5 Creating a Form Validation Ajax Application

In this section we shall modify the example GWT application to create a Catalog Form that is used to create a catalog entry in a HashMap. The Catalog form consists of input fields CatalogID, Journal, Publisher, Edition, Title, Author and Ajax is used for dynamic validation of the CatalogID field.

First, we need to modify the host HTML page, *C:\GWT\gwt-windows-1.4.60\src\com\gwt\public\CatalogForm.html*, to add DOM elements for labels and input text boxes to the HTML table. Add a button to submit the table and a DOM element for the validation message for the Catalog ID field. If a new Catalog ID is already in the HashMap, a validation message, "Catalog Id is not Valid", gets displayed, the text fields get filled with element values for the specified Catalog Id and the submit button gets disabled. If the Catalog ID specified is not in the HashMap a new entry is added to the HashMap. The modified <table/> element in *CatalogForm.html* is listed below.

```
<table align=center>
    <tr>
      <td id="label1"></td><td id="textBox1"></td>
    </tr>
    <tr>
      <td id="label2"></td><td id="textBox2"></td>
</tr>
  <tr>
      <td id="label3"></td><td id="textBox3"></td>
    </tr>
    <tr>
      <td id="label4"></td><td id="textBox4"></td>
</tr>
  <tr>
    <td id="label5"></td><td id="textBox5"></td>
</tr><tr>
    <td id="label6"></td><td id="textBox6"></td>
    </tr><tr>
    <td id="button"></td><td id="label7"></td>
    </tr></table>
```

Copy the modified table element to the table element in *CatalogForm.html* in JDeveloper. We also need to modify the *CatalogForm.java* class to validate a Catalog ID value. To the onModuleLoad() method add declarations for Label widgets for CatalogID, Journal, Publisher, Edition, Title, Author. Example of a Label component is as follows.

```
final Label label1 = new Label("Catalog ID");
```

A TextBox widgets to input values for a catalog entry. Example of a TextBox is as follows.

```
final TextBox textBox1 = new TextBox();
```

Add a Button widget to create a catalog entry.

```
final Button button = new Button("Submit");
```

Add the Label, TextBox, and Button widgets to the RootPanel. Example of adding a Label, a TextBox and button are as follows.

```
RootPanel.get("label1").add(label1);
RootPanel.get("textBox1").add(textBox1);
RootPanel.get("button").add(button);
```

Create a HashMap for catalog entries and add an initial set of catalog entries using an ArrayList for each catalog entry. An example ArrayList for a catalog entry is added as follows.

```
HashMap catalogHashMap=new  HashMap();
ArrayList arrayList= new  ArrayList();
arrayList.add(0, "catalog1");
arrayList.add(1, "Oracle Magazine");
arrayList.add(2, "Oracle Publishing");
arrayList.add(3, "May-June 2006");
arrayList.add(4, "Tuning Your View Objects");
arrayList.add(5, "Steve Muench");
```

Add a KeyboardListener to the TextBox for Catalog ID using a KeyboardListenerAdapter; if a KeyboardListenerAdapter is used not all the methods of the KeyboardListener interface have to be implemented. Implement only the onKeyUp() method.

```
textBox1.addKeyboardListener(new
KeyboardListenerAdapter() {
public void onKeyUp(Widget sender, char keyCode,
int modifiers) {
}
```

Add a ClickListener to the button and implement the onClick() method.

```
button.addClickListener(new ClickListener() {
public void onClick(Widget sender) {
  }
}
```

When a character is added to the TextBox for Catalog ID, the onKeyUp() method of the KeyboardListener gets invoked. Retrieve the text for the TextBox and check if a catalog entry for the specified Catalog ID already define in the HashMap. If a catalog entry for the Catalog ID is already defined, retrieve the values for the catalog entry and set the values in the host HTML page table DOM elements. Set the validation message to "Catalog ID is not Valid", and disable the submit button.

```
String catalogId = textBox1.getText();
 if(catalogHashMap.containsKey(catalogId))
 {
ArrayList
arraylist=(ArrayList)catalogHashMap.get(catalogId);
 label7.setText("Catalog Id is not Valid");
textBox2.setText((String)arraylist.get(1));
button.setEnabled(false);
 }
```

If the Catalog ID is not already defined in the HashMap, set the validation message indicating that the Catalog ID is valid, set the table field values to empty string and enable the Submit button.

```
label7.setText("Catalog Id is Valid");
textBox2.setText("");
button.setEnabled(true);
```

To create a new catalog entry specify values for the different rows of the catalog form and click on the Submit button. When the Submit button is clicked the onClick() method of the ClickListener gets invoked. In the onClick() method, retrieve the values in the different TextBoxes, create an ArrayList for a catalog entry and add a catalog entry to the HashMap.

```
String catalogId = textBox1.getText();
ArrayList arrayList= new  ArrayList();
  arrayList.add(0, catalogId);
  arrayList.add(1, textBox2.getText());
catalogHashMap.put(catalogId,arrayList);
```

The modified *CatalogForm.java* class is listed below.

```
package com.gwt.client;

import com.google.gwt.core.client.EntryPoint;
import com.google.gwt.user.client.ui.Button;
import com.google.gwt.user.client.ui.TextBox;
import com.google.gwt.user.client.ui.ClickListener;
```

```
import com.google.gwt.user.client.ui.Label;
import com.google.gwt.user.client.ui.RootPanel;
import com.google.gwt.user.client.ui.Widget;
import
com.google.gwt.user.client.ui.KeyboardListenerAdapter
;
import java.util.*;
import java.lang.Exception;

/**
 *       Entry      point      classes      define
<code>onModuleLoad()</code>.
 */
public class CatalogForm implements EntryPoint {
    /**
     * This is the entry point method.
     */
ArrayList arrayList;
HashMap catalogHashMap;
public void onModuleLoad() {
final Button button = new Button("Submit");
final Label label1 = new Label("Catalog ID");
final Label label2 = new Label("Journal");
final Label label3 = new Label("Publisher");
final Label label4 = new Label("Edition");
final Label label5 = new Label("Title");
final Label label6 = new Label("Author");
final Label label7 = new Label();
final TextBox textBox1 = new TextBox();
final TextBox textBox2 = new TextBox();
final TextBox textBox3 = new TextBox();
final TextBox textBox4 = new TextBox();
final TextBox textBox5 = new TextBox();
final TextBox textBox6 = new TextBox();
arrayList = new ArrayList();
arrayList.add(0, "catalog1");
arrayList.add(1, "Oracle Magazine");
arrayList.add(2, "Oracle Publishing");
arrayList.add(3, "May-June 2006");
arrayList.add(4, "Tuning Your View Objects");
arrayList.add(5, "Steve Muench");
catalogHashMap = new HashMap();
catalogHashMap.put("catalog1", arrayList);
arrayList = new ArrayList();
arrayList.add(0, "catalog2");
arrayList.add(1, "Oracle Magazine");
arrayList.add(2, "Oracle Publishing");
```

```
arrayList.add(3, "July-August 2006");
arrayList.add(4, "Evolving Grid Management");
arrayList.add(5, "David Baum");
catalogHashMap.put("catalog2", arrayList);
 textBox1.addKeyboardListener(new
 KeyboardListenerAdapter() {
    public   void   onKeyUp(Widget   sender,   char
    keyCode, int modifiers) {
try {
      String catalogId = textBox1.getText();
    if (catalogHashMap.containsKey(catalogId))
      {
       ArrayList arraylist =
       (ArrayList)catalogHashMap.get(catalogId);
       label7.setText("Catalog Id is not Valid");

textBox2.setText((String)arraylist.get(1));
textBox3.setText((String)arraylist.get(2));
textBox4.setText((String)arraylist.get(3));
textBox5.setText((String)arraylist.get(4));
textBox6.setText((String)arraylist.get(5));
button.setEnabled(false);
}
  else {
label7.setText("Catalog Id is Valid");
textBox2.setText("");
textBox3.setText("");
textBox4.setText("");
textBox5.setText("");
textBox6.setText("");
button.setEnabled(true);
  }
  } catch (Exception e) {
  }
    }
});
button.addClickListener(new ClickListener() {
  public void onClick(Widget sender) {
  String catalogId = textBox1.getText();
  arrayList = new ArrayList();
  arrayList.add(0, catalogId);
  arrayList.add(1, textBox2.getText());
  arrayList.add(2, textBox3.getText());
  arrayList.add(3, textBox4.getText());
  arrayList.add(4, textBox5.getText());
  arrayList.add(5, textBox6.getText());
  catalogHashMap.put(catalogId, arrayList);
```

```
}});
RootPanel.get("label1").add(label1);
RootPanel.get("label2").add(label2);
RootPanel.get("label3").add(label3);
RootPanel.get("label4").add(label4);
RootPanel.get("label5").add(label5);
RootPanel.get("label6").add(label6);
RootPanel.get("textBox1").add(textBox1);
RootPanel.get("textBox2").add(textBox2);
RootPanel.get("textBox3").add(textBox3);
RootPanel.get("textBox4").add(textBox4);
RootPanel.get("textBox5").add(textBox5);
RootPanel.get("textBox6").add(textBox6);
RootPanel.get("button").add(button);
RootPanel.get("label7").add(label7);}}
```

Copy the *CatalogForm.java* listing to the *CatalogForm.java* class in JDeveloper. Next, we shall run the GWT application in hosted mode. We need to set the runtime configuration to the hosted mode as shown in Fig. 4.16.

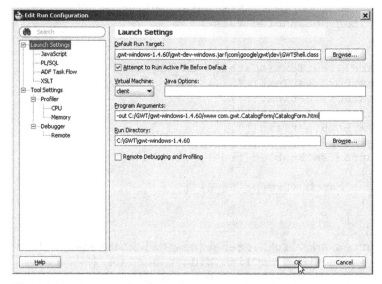

Fig. 4.16 Setting Run Configuration to Hosted Mode

Right-click on the GWT Web Project in the **Application Navigator** and select **Run** as shown in Fig. 4.17.

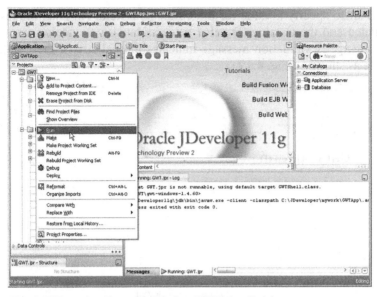

Fig. 4.17 Running Form Validation GWT Application

The HTML host page gets displayed. The HTML host page consists of a table containing rows for input values for a catalog entry and a **Submit** button as shown in Fig. 4.18.

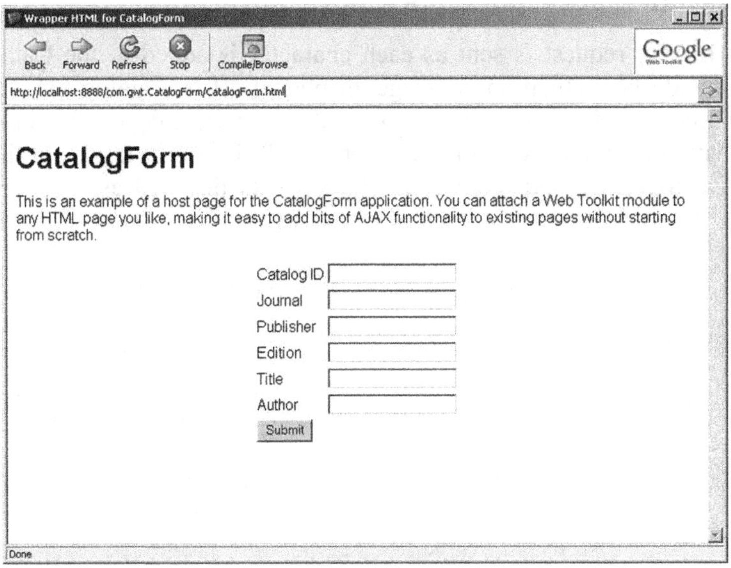

Fig. 4.18 Input Form for creating a Catalog Entry

Start to specify a value for the Catalog ID field. An Ajax request gets initiated and the Catalog ID value gets validated with catalog entries in a HashMap. A validation message indicates the validity of the Catalog ID value as shown in Fig. 4.19.

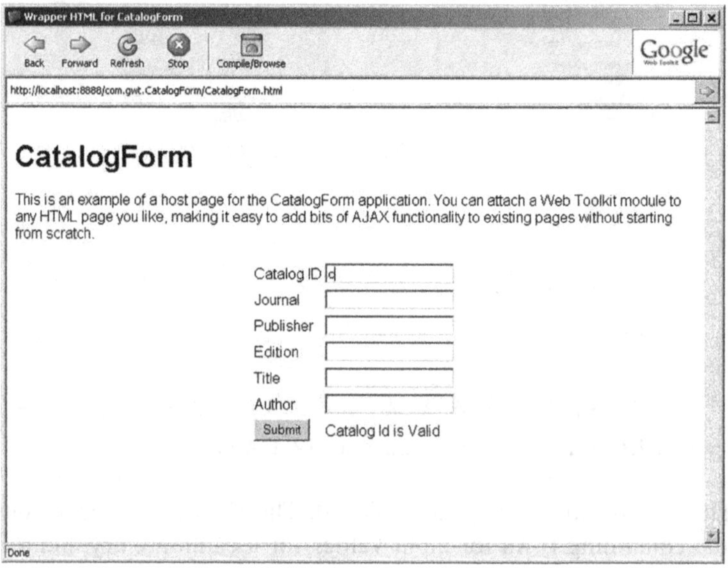

Fig. 4.19 Validating Catalog Id

An Ajax request is sent as each character is added to the Catalog ID field and the validation message displayed. If a Catalog ID value is specified that is already in the HashMap, catalog1 for example, a validation message: "Catalog Id is not Valid". The form fields get filled for the catalog entry and the **Submit** button gets disabled as shown in Fig. 4.20.

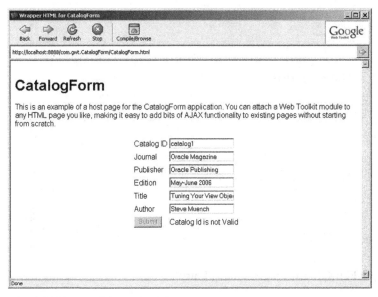

Fig. 4.20 Non Valid Catalog Id

If a Catalog ID is specified that is not already in the `HashMap`, a validation message gets displayed, "Catalog Id is valid". The form fields get set to empty fields and the **Submit** button gets enabled. Specify values for a catalog entry and click on the **Submit** button as shown in Fig. 4.21. A new catalog entry gets created in the `HashMap`.

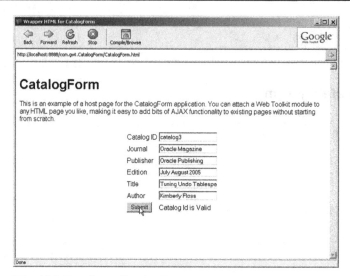

Fig. 4.21 Creating a Catalog Entry

If the Catalog ID value for which a new catalog entry is created is specified in the Catalog ID field again, the validation message indicates that the Catalog ID is not valid as shown in Fig. 4.22.

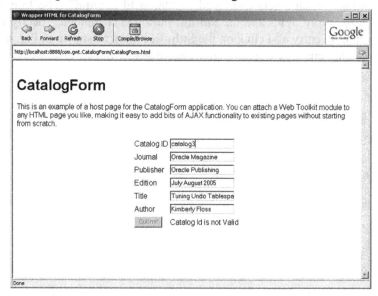

Fig. 4.22 A Catalog Id becomes Non Valid after a Catalog Entry is created

4.6 Summary

The Google Web Toolkit is an Ajax framework for Java and also provides a set of user interface components (widgets). A JRE emulation library is also included in GWT. A limitation of GWT is that by default only the Java classes in the JRE emulation library may be used in a GWT application. For example, if a JDBC connection with a database is to be created in a GWT application using the `java.sql` library, the Java-to-JavaScript compiler does not compile the Java class and generates an error.

5 Ajax with Java-DWR

5.1 Introduction

Direct Web Remoting (DWR) is a Java open source library for developing Ajax applications. DWR consists of two components: JavaScript running in the browser that sends requests and dynamically updates the web page with the response, and a Servlet running on the server that processes requests and sends response back to the browser. Remoting in DWR implies that Java class methods are remoted as JavaScript functions in the browser. DWR dynamically generates JavaScript corresponding to Java classes and the JavaScript may be run in the browser just as any other JavaScript class library. The JavaScript functions generated corresponding to Java class methods have a callback function as one of the parameters. The remote methods are invoked in the browser using a callback function and the request is sent to the server using Ajax. When the request is complete a response is returned to the browser using Ajax. The callback function specified in the remote method gets invoked with the data returned from the server and the web page may be updated with the server response.

5.2 Setting the Environment

Download the DWR[1] 1.1.4 JAR file *dwr.jar*. DWR is supported on most browsers. We shall be using Internet Explorer 6. DWR requires JDK 1.3 or later and a servlet container that support servlet specification 2.2 or later. Install a JDK if not already installed. JDK 1.5.0_13 was used in this chapter. DWR has been tested on the following web servers: Tomcat, WebLogic, WebSphere, JBoss, Jetty, Resin, Sun ONE, and Glassfish. We

---

[1] Download DWR-http://getahead.org/dwr

shall be using JBoss 4.x[2]; install JBoss 4.x if not already installed. We shall be using MySQL[3] database as the database for the DWR application, therefore, install MySQL 5.0. Create a database table `UserTable` in the MySQL database using the following script.

```
CREATE TABLE UserTable(userid VARCHAR(25)
PRIMARY KEY, password VARCHAR(25));
INSERT INTO UserTable VALUES('dvohra', 'ajaxdwr');
INSERT INTO UserTable VALUES('jsmith', 'smith');
```

Next, configure JBoss with MySQL. Copy the `mysql-ds.xml` file from the *C:\JBoss\jboss-4.2.2.GA\docs\examples\jca* directory to the *C:\JBoss\jboss-4.2.2.GA\server\default\deploy* directory. In the `mysql-ds.xml` file the MySQL datasource is specified as `MySqlDS`. Specify the connection URL and driver class as follows.

```
<connection-
url>jdbc:mysql://localhost:3306/test</connection-url>
<driver-class>com.mysql.jdbc.Driver</driver-class>
```

A password is not required for the root user. Specify user-name and password as follows.

```
<user-name>root</user-name>
<password></password>
```

Download the MySQL JDBC driver[4] JAR file *mysql-connector-java-5.1.5-bin.jar* and copy   the   JAR file   to   the   *C:\JBoss\jboss-4.2.2.GA\server\default\lib* directory. We shall be developing a DWR web application in JDeveloper 11g IDE. Download JDeveloper 11g zip. Extract the zip file to a directory and JDeveloper gets installed.

5.3 Creating a DWR Application

We shall be developing an Ajax registration form validation application to validate a userid. The form validation application is used to create user registration with a unique userid. If the User Id specified is not in the database table `UserTable` a message "User Id is valid" gets displayed and a new user registration entry may be created. If the User Id is already in the database a validation message, "User Id is not Valid" gets displayed.

---

[2] Download JBoss 4.x-http://www.jboss.org/products/jbossas
[3] Download MySQL 5.0-http://www.mysql.com/
[4]Download MySQL Connector/J JDBC
 Driver-http://www.mysql.com/products/connector/j/

First, create a JDeveloper application and project with **File>New**. In the **New Gallery** window select **General** in **Categories** and **Application** in **Items**. Specify an application name, DWRApp for example, and click on **OK**. Specify a project name, DWR, and click on **OK**. A JDeveloper application and project get created. Next create a JSP with **File>New**. In the **New Gallery** window select **Web Tier>JSP** in **Categories** and **JSP** in **Items**. Click on **OK**. In the **Create JSP** window specify **File Name** as *userregistration.jsp* and click on **OK**. The JSP shall be used to specify an HTML form and JavaScript functions to send an Ajax request. Next, create a Java class that is to be remoted with DWR generated JavaScript. Select **File>New** and subsequently select **General** in **Categories** and **Java Class** in **Items** in the **New Gallery** window. Click on **OK**. In the **Create Java Class** window specify a Java class **Name** as UserRegistration, and **Package** name as dwr and click on **OK**. A Java class gets added to the JDeveloper application. Next, we need to add a DWR configuration file *dwr.xml* in the WEB-INF directory. Select the WEB-INF folder in the **Application Navigator** and select **File>New**. In the **New Gallery** window select **General>XML** in **Categories** and **XML Document** in **Items** and click on **OK**. In the **Create XML File** window specify file name as *dwr.xml* and click on **OK**. A *dwr.xml* file gets created. Create a directory called *lib* in the WEB-INF directory and copy the *dwr.jar* file to the *lib* directory. The directory structure of the DWR application and project is shown in Fig. 5.1.

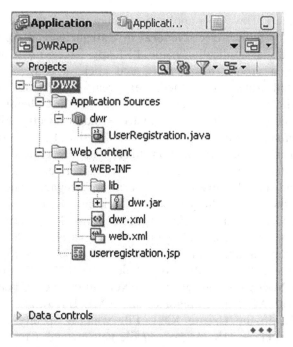

Fig. 5.1 DWR Application Structure

Next, we shall configure a connection with the JBoss application server. Select **View>Application Server Navigator** to display the **Application Server Navigator**. In the Application Server Navigator right-click on the DWRApp node and select New Application Server Connection as shown in Fig. 5.2.

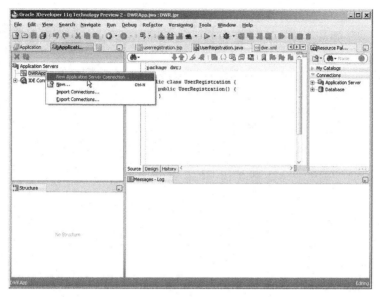

Fig. 5.2 Creating a New Application Server Connection

The **Application Server Connection Wizard** gets started. Click on **Next**. Specify **Connection Name** as JBossConnection, and select **Connection Type** as **JBoss 4.x**. Click on **Next** as shown in Fig. 5.3.

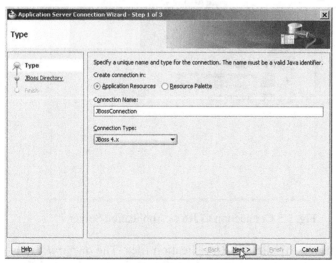

Fig. 5.3 Selecting Connection Type

In the **JBoss Directory** window **Host** is specified as localhost. Specify the deploy directory and click on **Next** as shown in Fig. 5.4.

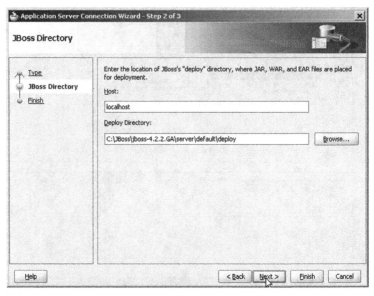

Fig. 5.4 Specifying Deploy Directory

Click on **Finish**. A JBoss application server connection gets created as shown in Fig. 5.5.

Fig. 5.5 Connection to JBoss Application Server

We shall modify the DWR application files. The *dwr.xml* file is used to specify creators and converters. The DTD[5] for the *dwr.xml* file may be used to create a *dwr.xml* file. The root element of the *dwr.xml* file is dwr.

---

[5] DTD for dwr.xml-http://getahead.org/dwr/dwr10.dtd

Creators are used to create JavaScript corresponding to Java classes and converters are used to convert between Java data types on the server-side and JavaScript data types on the client-side. Data types `boolean`, `byte`, `short`, `int`, `long`, `float`, `double`, `char`, `java.lang.Boolean`, `java.lang.Byte`, `java.lang.Short`, `java.lang.Integer`, `java.lang.Long`, `java.lang.Float`, `java.lang.Double`, `java.lang.Character`, `java.math.BigInteger`, `java.math.BigDecimal` and `java.lang.String` and the date converter are enabled by default. Therefore, we won't be specifying a converter. Classes that are to be allowed access from JavaScript are specified in the `allow` element. The `create` element specifies the classes that are to be remoted in JavaScript.

```
<!ELEMENT allow (
    (create | convert)*
)>
```

The `create` element has required attributes `creator` and `javascript` and an optional attribute `scope`.

```
<!ATTLIST create
    creator CDATA #REQUIRED
    javascript CDATA #REQUIRED
    scope (application|session|request|page) #IMPLIED
>
```

The `creator` attribute specifies which creator is used to instantiate the Java class. The most commonly used creator is "new". The `javascript` attribute specifies the JavaScript class library that is created from the Java class. The `scope` attribute specifies the scope in which the Java bean is available and may be set to "application", "page", "session" and "request". The `scope` attribute is optional and the default value is "page". Specify the `create` element for the example application as follows.

```
<allow>
    <create creator="new"
javascript="UserRegistration">
        <param name="class"
value="dwr.UserRegistration"/>
    </create>
  </allow>
```

The `create` element has 0 or more each of `param`, `include`, `exclude` and `auth` sub-elements.

```
<!ELEMENT create (
    (param | include | exclude | auth)*)>
```

The `param` element is used to specify configuration for different type of creators. The "new" creator requires the type of object to invoke new on. For example, to invoke `new` on Java class `UserRegistration` we used a `param` element.

```
<param name="class" value="dwr.UserRegistration"/>
```

The `include` element specifies which methods are to be included for remoting in JavaScript. The default is all methods. The `exclude` element specifies which Java class methods are excluded for remoting. By default none of the methods are excluded. Copy *dwr.xml* to the JDeveloper project. The *dwr.xml* for the example DWR application is shown below.

```
<!DOCTYPE dwr PUBLIC
    "-//GetAhead Limited//DTD Direct Web Remoting
1.0//EN"
    "http://www.getahead.ltd.uk/dwr/dwr10.dtd">
<dwr>
  <allow>
  <create creator="new" javascript=
"UserRegistration">
    <param name="class" value="dwr.UserRegistration"/>
    </create>
    </allow>
</dwr>
```

We also need to modify the `web.xml` deployment descriptor to specify the `DWRServlet`.The DWR servlet class for DWR 1.1.4 is `uk.ltd.getahead.dwr.DWRServlet`. The DWR servlet class for DWR 2.x is `org.directwebremoting.servlet.DwrServlet`. Copy `web.xml`, which is listed below, to the JDeveloper project.

```
<?xml version = '1.0' encoding = 'windows-1252'?>
<web-app  xmlns:xsi=http://www.w3.org/2001/XMLSchema-
instance
xsi:schemaLocation="http://java.sun.com/xml/ns/j2ee
http://java.sun.com/xml/ns/j2ee/web-app_2_4.xsd"
          version="2.4"
xmlns="http://java.sun.com/xml/ns/j2ee">
    <description>Empty    web.xml    file    for    Web
Application</description>
    <servlet>
        <display-name>DWR Servlet</display-name>
        <servlet-name>dwr-invoker</servlet-name>
        <servlet-
        class>uk.ltd.getahead.dwr.DWRServlet
        </servlet-class>
```

```
    <init-param>
        <param-name>debug</param-name>
        <param-value>true</param-value>
    </init-param>
</servlet>
<servlet-mapping>
    <servlet-name>dwr-invoker</servlet-name>
    <url-pattern>/dwr/*</url-pattern>
</servlet-mapping>
<session-config>
    <session-timeout>35</session-timeout>
</session-config>
<mime-mapping>
    <extension>html</extension>
    <mime-type>text/html</mime-type>
</mime-mapping>
<mime-mapping>
    <extension>txt</extension>
    <mime-type>text/plain</mime-type>
</mime-mapping>
</web-app>
```

The Java class to be remoted, UserRegistration.java, specifies two methods validate(String userId) and updateUserTable(String userId, String password). The validate method validates a User Id specified in the user registration entry form. The return type of the validate method is boolean. In the validate method, first a connection with MySQL database is obtained using datasource configured in JBoss.

```
InitialContext        initialContext      =        new
InitialContext();
javax.sql.DataSource ds =
(javax.sql.DataSource)initialContext.lookup("java:My
SqlDS");
java.sql.Connection conn = ds.getConnection();
```

A SQL query is run in the MySQL database using the User Id specified in the user registration entry form.

```
Statement stmt = conn.createStatement();
String query =
        "SELECT  *  from  UserTable  WHERE  userId="  +
"'" + userId + "'";
ResultSet rs = stmt.executeQuery(query);
```

If the result set is not empty the User Id specified is already defined in the database and is therefore not valid. The business logic of what is a valid user id may contain match with a regular expression pattern. We have used the business logic that if a user id is not already defined the user id is valid. If the result set has data set the value of a `boolean` variable to `false`.

```
if (rs.next()) {
    valid  = false;
    return valid;
}
```

If the result set is empty the User Id is valid and a new user registration entry may be created. Return `true` if the result set is empty. If the User Id is valid the `updateUserTable` method is invoked to create a new user entry. Copy `UserRegistration.java`, which is listed below, to the JDeveloper project.

```
package dwr;

import java.sql.*;
import javax.naming.InitialContext;
public class UserRegistration {
public UserRegistration() {
    }
    public boolean validate(String userId) {
        boolean valid=true;
        try {
            InitialContext initialContext =
            new InitialContext();
            javax.sql.DataSource ds =
          (javax.sql.DataSource)initialContext.lookup
          ("java:MySqlDS");
            java.sql.Connection conn
              = ds.getConnection();
            // Obtain result set
            Statement stmt = conn.createStatement();
            String query =
            "SELECT * from UserTable WHERE userId="
            + "'" + userId +
                "'";
            ResultSet rs = stmt.executeQuery(query);
            if (rs.next()) {
              valid = false;
              return valid;
            }
            conn.close();
        } catch (SQLException e) {
            System.out.println(e.getMessage());
```

```
      } catch (javax.naming.NamingException e) {
         System.out.println(e.getMessage());
      }
        return valid;
   }
    public  String  updateUserTable(String  userId,
   String password) {
      try {
         InitialContext initialContext =
         new InitialContext();
         javax.sql.DataSource ds =
         (javax.sql.DataSource)initialContext.lookup
          ("java:MySqlDS");
         java.sql.Connection          conn          =
         ds.getConnection();
         Statement stmt = conn.createStatement();
         String sql =
         "INSERT INTO UserTable VALUES(" + "\'" +
         userId + "\'" + "," +
            "\'" + password + "\'" + ")";
         stmt.execute(sql);
         conn.close();
      } catch (SQLException e) {
         System.out.println(e.getMessage());
      } catch (javax.naming.NamingException e) {
         System.out.println(e.getMessage());
      }
        return null;
   }
 }
```

The JavaScript functions and the user registration entry form are specified in the *userregistration.jsp* file. First, we need to include the JavaScript file created from the Java class `UserRegistration` in *userregistration.jsp*. The JavaScript file for the `UserRegistration` class was specified as `UserRegistration` in *dwr.xml*. Include the `UserRegistration.js` as follows.

```
<scripttype='text/javascript'
src='/webapp1/dwr/interface/ UserRegistration.js'>
</script>
```

`Webapp1` specifies the web application WAR file, which we shall create from the DWR application later in the section. We also need to include `engine.js` and `util.js` in *userregistration.jsp*. `Engine.js` is required to marshall invocations from the dynamically generated

JavaScript functions for the Java class methods. In `engine.js` a DWR engine is created as follows.

```
var DWREngine = dwr.engine;
```

The DWR engine may be used to specify options such as timeout or specify handlers such as `errorHandler`, `exceptionHandler`, and callback handler. The `util.js` JavaScript file contains functions to update a web page using data returned by the server. Some of the commonly used `util.js` functions are discussed in Table 5.1.

Table 5.1 util.js Functions

Function	Description
$()	Retrieves an element by id. Equivalent of document.getElementById
getText(id)	Returns the displayed text for a select list.
getValue(id)	Returns the value of an element.
getValues()	Returns values for a JavaScript object that contains a collection of name/value pairs. The name/value pairs are the element ids and their values.
setValue(id, value)	Sets value of an element.
setValues()	Sets values of a collection of name/value pairs representing element ids and their values.

In *userregistration.jsp* create a HTML table that consists of fields for User Id and Password. The User Id field value is validated as the value is specified using the `onkeyup` event handler. Invoke the JavaScript function `validateUserId` with the `onkeyup` function.

```
<table>
    <tr>
      <td>User ID:</td>
      <td>
        <input id="userId"
          type="text" onkeyup="validateUserId()"/>
      </td>
    </tr>
</table>
```

In the `validateUserId` function retrieve the value of the `userId` field and invoke the remote method `validate` using a callback function as an argument to the method. The callback function may be specified as the first parameter or the last parameter. The callback function is recommended to be the specified as the last parameter, but some of the examples on the DWR web site specify the callback function as the first parameter. We shall also specify the callback unction as the first parameter. The `validate` method is invoked with callback function `getValMessage` and the `userId` value.

```
function validateUserId(){
  var userId = DWRUtil.getValue("userId");
  UserRegistration.validate(getValMessage, userId);
  }
```

The callback function may also be specified as a call meta-data object.

```
UserRegistration.validate(userId, {
callback:function(msg) { }
});
```

When the Ajax request is complete the callback function `getValMessage` gets invoked with the `boolean` returned by the `validate` method as an argument. In the `getValMessage` callback function, if the `boolean` returned is `true` implying that the User Id is not defined in the database display the validation message "User ID is valid". If the `boolean` is `false` display the validation message "User ID is not valid". If the User Id is valid specify the Password field and submit the user entry with the **Submit** button, which invokes the `addUserRegistration()` JavaScript function. In the `addUserRegistration()` function retrieve the values for the different form fields and invoke the remote method `updateUserTable` with a callback function and the field values as parameters. In the Java class method `updateUserTable` obtain a connection with the MySQL database and create a user entry. The callback function `clearForm` clears the user entry form. The *userregistration.jsp* is listed below.

```
<!DOCTYPE  HTML   PUBLIC   "-//W3C//DTD  HTML  4.01
Transitional//EN"
"http://www.w3.org/TR/html4/loose.dtd">
<%@    page    contentType="text/html;charset=windows-
1252"%>
<html>
  <head>
    <meta                     http-equiv="Content-Type"
content="text/html; charset=windows-1252"/>
    <title>userregistration</title>
  </head>
  <body>
  <script type='text/javascript'
    src='/webapp1/dwr/interface/
  UserRegistration.js'>
  </script><script type='text/javascript'
    src='/webapp1/dwr/engine.js'></script>
```

```
<script type='text/javascript'
src='/webapp1/dwr/util.js'>
</script><script type='text/javascript'>
 function addUserRegistration(){
  var userId = DWRUtil.getValue("userId");
  var password = DWRUtil.getValue("password");
  UserRegistration.updateUserTable(clearForm,
userId, password);
  }
function  validateUserId(){
  var userId = DWRUtil.getValue("userId");
  UserRegistration.validate(getValMessage,
userId);
  }
 function getValMessage(msg){
  if(msg==true){
  DWRUtil.setValue("validationMsg","User    ID    is
valid");
  }else{
  DWRUtil.setValue("validationMsg","User ID is not
valid");
  }
  }
 function clearForm(msg){
  DWRUtil.setValue("userId","");
  DWRUtil.setValue("password","");

  DWRUtil.setValue("validationMsg","");
  }
</script><table>
     <tr>
      <td>User ID:</td>
      <td>
       <input         id="userId"        type="text"
       onkeyup="validateUserId()"/>
       </td>
      </tr>
      <tr>
        <td>Password:</td>
        <td>
          <input id="password" type="text"/>
        </td>
      </tr>
      <tr>
        <td>
          <input      id="button1"     type="button"
value="Submit" onclick="addUserRegistration()"/>
```

```
          </td>
          <td>  <div  id="validationMsg"> </div></td>
          </tr>
        </table>
      </body>
  </html>
```

The JavaScript has been specified in the JSP, but the JavaScript may also be specified in a separate JavaScript file and the JavaScript file included in the JSP with a `<script/>` tag. Copy *userregistration.jsp* to the JDeveloper DWR application.

5.4 Deploying and Running the DWR Application

Next, we need to create a web application from the DWR application and deploy the web application to JBoss server using the connection we created earlier. To create a WAR File deployment profile select **File>New** and subsequently **General>Deployment Profiles** in the **New Gallery** window in **Categories**. Select **WAR File** in **Items** and click on **OK**. In the **Create Deployment Profile** window specify **Deployment Profile Name** as webapp1 and click on **OK**. Click on **OK** in the **WAR Deployment Profile Properties** window. A deployment profile gets created and gets listed in the **Project Properties** window in the **Deployment** node. To deploy the WAR file deployment profile to JBoss right-click on the DWR project in **Application Navigator** and select **Deploy>webapp1>to>JBossConnection** as shown in Fig. 5.6.

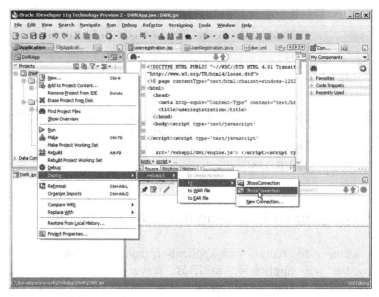

Fig. 5.6 Deploying DWR Application to JBoss Server

A WAR file `webapp1` gets deployed to the `deploy` directory of the default server. Start the JBoss server with the `run` batch file in the *C:\JBoss\jboss-4.2.2.GA\bin* directory. Invoke the *userregistration.jsp* with the URL `http://localhost:8080/webapp1/` `userregistration.jsp`. Start to specify a User Id value. The User Id value gets modified with each modification to the User Id field and a validation message gets displayed as shown in Fig 5.7. Single-character user IDs are not typically used. The business logic of what is and what is not a valid user ID can be specified on the server side. In addition to testing if a user ID entry has been already specified in the database business logic can be added to check the length of the user ID and whether or not it starts with a particular character.

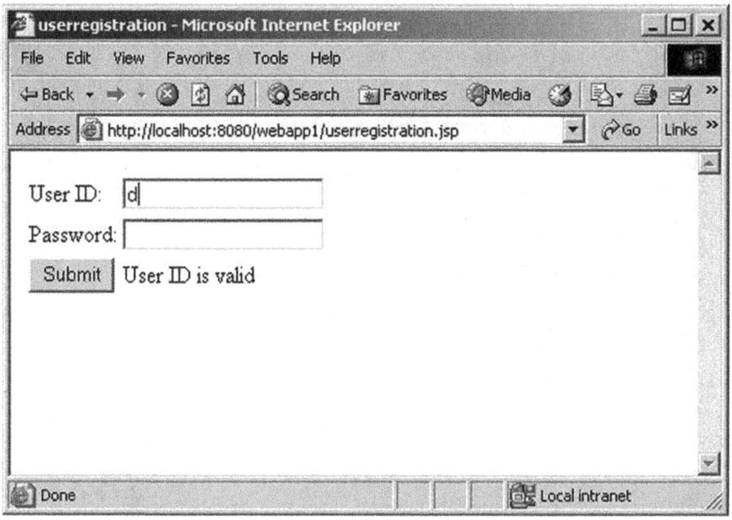

Fig. 5.7 Validating User Id

If a valid User Id is specified validation message "User Id is Valid" gets displayed. If a User Id that is already defined in the database is specified a validation message "User Id is not Valid" gets displayed as shown in Fig. 5.8.

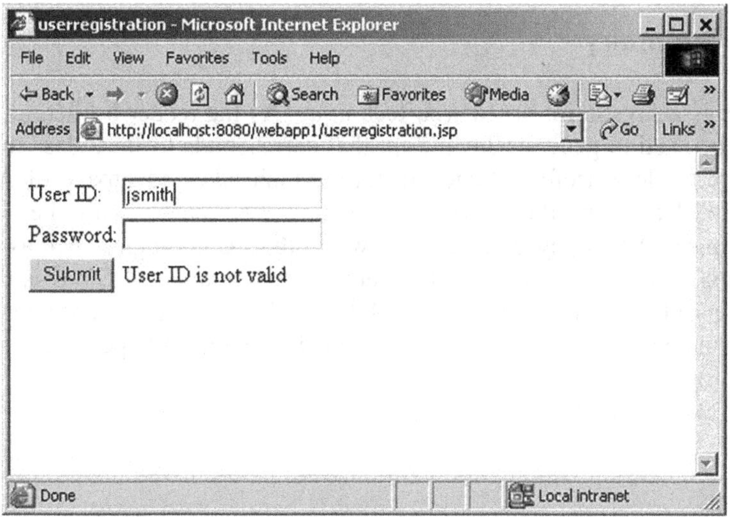

Fig. 5.8 Non Valid User Id

To create a new user registration specify a valid User Id, specify a password and click on the **Submit** button as shown in Fig. 5.9.

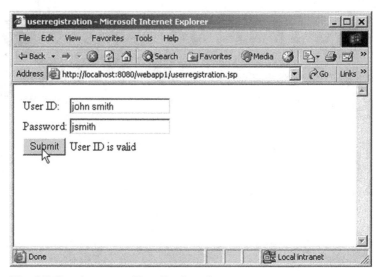

Fig. 5.9 Creating a new User Registration

A user entry gets created and the form fields get reset. If the same user Id is re-specified a validation message indicating that the User Id is not valid gets displayed.

5.5 Summary

Ajax is a JavaScript based web technique. As the reader has learnt, DWR can be used to generate JavaScript that corresponds to Java class methods that provide a useful callback feature, which takes advantage of Ajax to return data from the server and update web pages with the server's response. DWR may be integrated with other technologies such as Struts, Spring, JavaServer Faces, and Hibernate. A limitation of DWR is that the server-side application is required to be Java based. According to the Ajaxian.com[6] survey, DWR is used by about 12 percent of Ajax developers.

---

[6] Ajaxian survey-http://ajaxian.com/archives/ajaxiancom-2006-survey-results

6 Ajax without JavaScript – AjaxTags

6.1 Introduction

Asynchronous JavaScript and XML (Ajax) is a web technique used to transfer data between a client script running on a web page and a server without posting the web page to the server. In a chap. 1 we developed an Ajax application to validate a form as data is added to the form. An XMLHttpRequest object is used to send an HTTP request from a web page JavaScript and process the HTTP response from the server. If the reader is not familiar with JavaScript and would rather have a predefined JSP tag library provide the Ajax functionality, AjaxTags would be well suited to the reader's Ajax application requirements. AjaxTags is a JSP tag library for implementing the Ajax web technique in a JSP page. JavaScript code to create an XMLHttpRequest object, send a request and process the response is not required, because the Ajax web technique is implemented by AjaxTags.

6.2 Setting the Environment

We need to install a web server to develop the AjaxTags application. JDeveloper includes an embedded OC4J server. Therefore, install JDeveloper 11g. Also install the Oracle 10g database including a database instance, ORCL, and the sample schemas. Download the AjaxTags Binary zip file *ajaxtags-1.2-beta2-bin.zip*. Extract the zip file to a directory, *C:\AjaxTags* directory for example. Next, create an Oracle database table with the following SQL script.

```
CREATE TABLE OE.Catalog(CatalogId VARCHAR(25) PRIMARY
KEY,      Journal      VARCHAR(25),      Publisher
VARCHAR(25),Edition VARCHAR(25), Title Varchar(45),
Author Varchar(25));
```

```
INSERT  INTO  OE.Catalog  VALUES('catalog1',  'Oracle
Magazine',  'Oracle  Publishing',  'Nov-Dec  2004',
'Database Resource Manager', 'Kimberly Floss');

INSERT  INTO  OE.Catalog  VALUES('catalog2',  'Oracle
Magazine',   'Oracle  Publishing', 'Nov-Dec  2004',
'From ADF UIX to JSF', 'Jonas Jacobi');

INSERT  INTO  OE.Catalog  VALUES('catalog3',  'Oracle
Magazine',   'Oracle Publishing', 'March-April 2005',
'Starting with Oracle ADF ', 'Steve Muench');
```

Next, create a new application and project with **File>New**. In the **New Gallery** window select **General** in **Categories** and **Application** in **Items**. In the **Create Application** window specify an **Application Name** and click on **OK**. In the **Create Project** window specify a **Project Name** and click on **OK**. A new application and project get added as shown in Fig. 6.1.

Fig. 6.1 AjaxTags Application

Next, create a JDBC connection in JDeveloper with Oracle database. Select **View>Database Navigator** to display the **Database Navigator**. Right-click on the **AjaxTags** node and select **New Connection**, as shown in Fig. 6.2, to create a new database connection with Oracle database.

Fig. 6.2 Creating a New Connection

In the **Create Database Connection** window specify a **Connection Name** and select **Connection Type** as **Oracle (JDBC)**. Specify a **Username** and **Password** and specify **SID** as ORCL. Driver is the **thin** driver, **Hostname** is **localhost**, and **JDBC Port** is 1521 by default. Click on **Test Connection** to test the connection. If a connection gets established a "Success" message gets displayed. Click on **OK** as shown in Fig. 6.3.

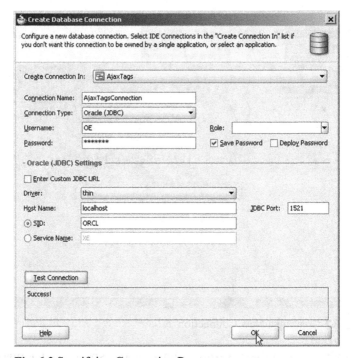

Fig. 6.3 Specifying Connection Parameters

An `AjaxTagsConnection` connection, which is available as a JNDI resource `jdbc/AjaxTagsConnectionDS`, gets added to the Database Navigator as shown in Fig. 6.4.

Fig. 6.4 Connection for AjaxTags Application

To the web.xml deployment descriptor we need to add the following resource-ref definition, which is required to access the data source from a web application.

```
<resource-ref>
<res-ref-name>jdbc/AjaxTagsConnectionDS</res-ref-
name><res-type>javax.sql.DataSource</res-type>
<res-auth>Container</res-auth>
</resource-ref>
```

6.3 Overview of AjaxTags

AjaxTags provides various tags to implement the Ajax functionality. Some of the commonly used tags are discussed in Table 6.1.

Table 6.1 AjaxTags Tags

Tag Name	Description	Parameters
ajax:anchors	Converts any anchor tags (<a></a> tags) to be AJAX enabled.	target(required)-Target region on the page where the AJAX response is output. ajaxFlag-A boolean flag to indicate if the rest of the page is to be ignored in an AJAX call (default value is false).
ajax:autocomplete	Retrieves a list of probable values from the server, for a incomplete text in an input field, and displays them in a dropdown beneath the input text field. The input text field gets autocompleted when a value is selected from the list.	baseUrl(required)-Server side url that processes the Ajax request and returns a list of values. source(required)-id of the text field in which the search string is specified. Value of autocomplete selection gets specified in this field. target(required)-id of the text field in which value of autocomplete selection gets specified. The target id may be set to the same value as the source id if a second field is not required to be filled with the autocomplete selection. parameters(required)-A list of parameters sent to the server.

Table 6.1 (continued)

Tag Name	Description	Parameters
ajax:htmlContent	Fills a region on the page with HTML content returned by the server. Tag should be after the web form.	baseUrl(required)-Server side url that processes the Ajax request. source-id of the element to which the event is attached. sourceClass-CSS class name to which event is attached. Either source or sourceClass is required. target(required)-id of div tag or other element that is filled with the HTML response. parameters(required)-A list of parameters sent to the server.
ajax:select	Retrieves a list of values from the server and displays them in a HTML select list. Tag is required to appear after the web form.	baseUrl(required)-Server side url that processes the Ajax request. source-id of the select field to which the event is attached. target(required)-id of the select field that is filled with the AJAX response. parameters(required)-A list of parameters sent to the server.
ajax:updateField	Updates one or more form fields based on value of another field.	baseUrl(required)-Server side url that processes the Ajax request. source-Form field whose value is sent to the server as a parameter. target(required)-A list of form field IDs that are filled with the AJAX response. action(required)-id of button or image tag that sends the onclick event.

6.4 Installing AjaxTags

In this section we shall create an AjaxTags application in JDeveloper. To
the AjaxTags project add a JSP page, *input.jsp*, with **File>New**. In the
New Gallery window select **Web Tier>JSP** in **Categories** and **JSP** in
Items and click on **OK**. Specify **File Name** in the **Create JSP** window
and click on **OK**. Similarly, add JSPs *error.jsp* for error message, and
catalog.jsp for success message. For server side processing add a servlet,
FormServlet, by selecting **Web Tier>Servlets** in **Categories** and
HTTP Servlet in **Items** in the **New Gallery** window. Click on **Next** in
Create HTTP Servlet window. In the **Servlet Information** window
specify **Class** as FormServlet and click on **Next**. In the **Mapping
Information** window specify **URL Pattern** as /formservlet and click
on **Next**. Click on **Finish** in the **Servlet Parameters** window. Similarly,
add another servlet FormUpdateServlet with **URL Pattern**
/formupdateservlet. Add JAR files *standard-1.0.6.jar, commons-
lang-2.1.jar* from the *lib* directory of the AjaxTags distribution and
ajaxtags-1.2-beta2.jar from the *dist* directory of the AjaxTags distribution
directory to the AjaxTags project libraries. To add the Jar files to the
project libraries select **Tools>Project Properties** and in the **Project
Properties** window select **Libraries** and add the JAR files with the **Add
Jar/Directory** button. Click on **OK** as shown in Fig. 6.5.

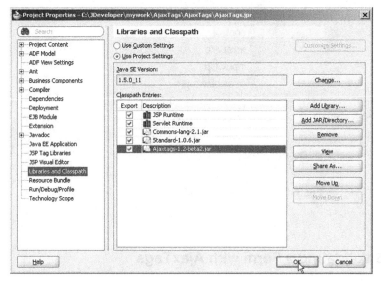

Fig. 6.5 AjaxTags Libraries

Copy JavaScript files *ajaxtags.js*, *overlibmws.js*, *prototype-1.4.0.js*, *scriptaculous.js* , and *controls.js* from the *js* directory of the AjaxTags distribution to the *public_html* directory of the AjaxTags project. We also need to copy *ajaxtags-1.2-beta2.jar* from the *dist* directory of AjaxTags binary distribution to *WEB-INF/lib* directory of the AjaxTags project in JDeveloper. The directory structure of the AjaxTags project is shown in Fig. 6.6.

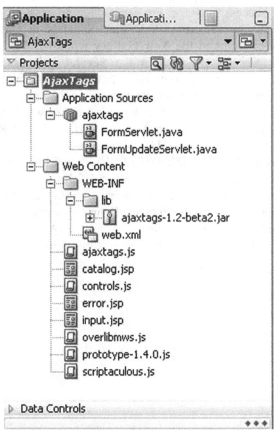

Fig. 6.6 AjaxTags Application Directory Structure

6.5 Validating a Form with AjaxTags

In this section we shall validate an input form that has a Catalog Id value as one of the inputs. The form is used to create a new catalog entry in the

Catalog table in the Oracle database. The Catalog Id value is selected from a list of values. A validation message indicates the validity of the Catalog Id value. The input form uses the AjaxTags tag library to send an Ajax request and process an Ajax response. JSP *input.jsp* is the input form. In *input.jsp* declare a taglib directive for the AjaxTags taglib.

```
<%@      taglib      uri="http://ajaxtags.org/tags/ajax"
prefix="ajax" %>
```

Specify the JavaScript files for AjaxTags in the *input.jsp*. JavaScript file *prototype-1.4.0.js* should be specified before the *ajaxtags.js*.

```
<script      type="text/javascript"      src="prototype-
1.4.0.js">
</script>
<script                          type="text/javascript"
src="scriptaculous.js">
</script>
<script type="text/javascript" src="overlibmws.js">
</script>
<script type="text/javascript" src="ajaxtags.js">
</script>
```

Add a selection list of values for Catalog Id and fields for Journal, Publisher, Edition, Title, and Author. Also add a div for the validationMessage. We shall use the ajax:htmlContent tag to validate a Catalog Id value. The ajax:htmlContent tag specifies a source attribute that specifies the form element that initiates an Ajax request. The baseUrl attribute specifies the URL to which the Ajax request is sent. The parameters attribute specifies the parameters to be sent with the Ajax request. The target attribute specifies the form element that is to be updated with the response from the server.

```
<ajax:htmlContent
  baseUrl="formservlet"
  source="catalogId"
  target="validationMessage"
  parameters="catalogId={catalogId}" />
```

In the example application the catalogId initiates an Ajax request, which gets sent to server URL formservlet with the GET method with parameters catalogId. The server HTML response updates the content of the validationMessage div. URL formservlet is mapped to FormServlet. In the doGet() method of the FormServlet retrieve the value of the catalogId.

```
String catalogId = request.getParameter("catalogId");
```

Obtain a JDBC connection with Oracle database using the datasource configured in JDeveloper with the database. Retrieve a result set for the Catalog Id. If the result set is empty the Catalog Id value specified in the input form is valid and if the result set is not empty the Catalog Id value is not valid. The business logic for defining a valid Catalog Id may include match with a regular expression pattern. The response from the server for an Ajax request sent with the `ajax:htmlContent` tag is required to be HTML. Therefore, set content type of the response to HTML.

```
response.setContentType("text/html");
```

With `rs` as the ResultSet output an HTML response that includes instructions about the validity of the Catalog Id value.

```
if (rs.next()) {
    out.println("<p>Catalog Id is not Valid</p>");
} else {
    out.println("<p>Catalog Id is Valid</p>");
}
```

For a valid catalog Id a new catalog entry may be created using the **Create Catalog Entry** button. The form is submitted using HTTP method POST, which invokes the `doPost()` method in the `FormServlet` servlet. In the `doPost()` method the field values in the input form are retrieved, a connection with the database obtained and a new catalog entry created. The `FormServlet.java` servlet class is listed below.

```
package ajaxtags;

import java.io.*;
import java.sql.*;
import javax.naming.InitialContext;
import javax.servlet.*;
import javax.servlet.http.*;

public class FormServlet extends HttpServlet {
    public void doGet(HttpServletRequest request,
                      HttpServletResponse response)
throws ServletException, IOException {
  try {
// Obtain value of Catalog Id field to ve validated.
String catalogId = request.getParameter("catalogId");
  if (catalogId.equals("Select Catalog Id")) {
    response.setContentType("text/html");
    response.setHeader("Cache-Control", "no-cache");
    PrintWriter out = response.getWriter();
    out.println("<p></p>");
```

```
    }
    if (!(catalogId.equals("Select Catalog Id"))) {
    // Obtain Connection
InitialContext initialContext = new InitialContext();
javax.sql.DataSource ds =
(javax.sql.DataSource)initialContext.lookup("java:com
p/env/jdbc/AjaxTagsConnectionDS");
java.sql.Connection conn = ds.getConnection();
    // Obtain result set
Statement stmt = conn.createStatement();
String query = "SELECT * from OE.Catalog WHERE
CatalogId=" + "'" + catalogId + "'";
ResultSet rs = stmt.executeQuery(query);
// set headers before accessing the Writer
response.setContentType("text/html");
response.setHeader("Cache-Control", "no-cache");
PrintWriter out = response.getWriter();
// then write the response
// If result set is empty set valid element to true
  if (rs.next()) {
      out.println("<p>Catalog Id is not Valid</p>");
  } else {
   out.println("<p>Catalog Id is Valid</p>");
                }
rs.close();
stmt.close();
conn.close();
}
  } catch (javax.naming.NamingException e) {
  } catch (SQLException e) {
  }
}
public void doPost(HttpServletRequest request,
        HttpServletResponse response) throws
ServletException, IOException {
  try {
        // Obtain Connection
InitialContext initialContext = new InitialContext();
javax.sql.DataSource ds =
(javax.sql.DataSource)initialContext.lookup("java:com
p/env/jdbc/AjaxTagsConnectionDS");
java.sql.Connection conn = ds.getConnection();
String catalogId = request.getParameter("catalogId");
String journal = request.getParameter("journal");
String publisher = request.getParameter("publisher");
String edition = request.getParameter("edition");
String title = request.getParameter("title");
```

```
String author = request.getParameter("author");
Statement stmt = conn.createStatement();
String sql = "INSERT INTO Catalog VALUES(" + "\'" +
catalogId + "\'" + "," +
                "\'" + journal + "\'" + "," + "\'" +
publisher + "\'" + "," +
                "\'" + edition + "\'" + "," + "\'" +
title + "\'" + "," +
                "\'" + author + "\'" + ")";
stmt.execute(sql);
response.sendRedirect("catalog.jsp");
stmt.close();
conn.close();
  } catch (javax.naming.NamingException e) {
    response.sendRedirect("error.jsp");
    } catch (SQLException e) {
     response.sendRedirect("error.jsp");
    }
  }
}
```

Copy FormServlet class to the FormServlets.java class in AjaxTags project in JDeveloper. Next, update the input form fields with catalog entry values for a Catalog Id for which a catalog entry is already defined in the database table.   Add an ajax:updateField tag to update form fields. The baseUrl attribute of the ajax:updateField tag specifies the server URL to which the Ajax request is sent. The source attribute specifies the form field that specifies the parameter to be sent with the Ajax request. The target attribute specifies a comma-separated list of form fields that are to be filled with response from the server. The action attribute specifies the ID of the form button or image that initiates an Ajax request. The parser attribute specifies the parser to be used to parse the server response. The default parser is ResponseHtmlParser. If the response is XML, set the parser to ResponseXmlParser. The parameters attribute specifies the list of parameters to be sent to the server.

```
<ajax:updateField
  baseUrl="formupdateservlet"
  source="catalogId"
  target="journal,publisher,edition,title,author"
  action="updateForm"
  parser="new ResponseXmlParser()"
  parameters="catalogId={catalogId}" />
```

In the example application the `baseUrl` is `formupdateservlet`. As `formupdateservlet` is mapped to `FormUpdateServlet` the Ajax request is sent to `FormUpdateServlet`. The `source` attribute is set to `catalogId` and the `parameters` attribute is also set to `catalogId`, the field value that is sent with the Ajax request. The `action` attribute is set to `updateForm`, a button ID in the form. The `target` attribute is set to `journal, publisher, edition,title, author`, and the form fields that are to be filled with the server response. The `parser` attribute is set to `ResponseXmlParser`.

In the `FormUpdateServlet`, the `catalogId` parameter value is retrieved and a result set obtained from the database table `Catalog` for the `catalogId` value. The XML response from the server is constructed with the `AjaxXmlBuilder` class. The format of the XML response is as follows.

```
<?xml version="1.0" encoding="UTF-8"?>
<ajax-response>
  <response>
    <item>
      <name>Record 1</name>
      <value>1</value>
    </item>
    <item>
      <name>Record 2</name>
      <value>2</value>
    </item>
    <item>
      <name>Record 3</name>
      <value>3</value>
    </item>
  </response>
</ajax-response>
```

Create an `AjaxXmlBuilder` object to construct the response and set the response content type to `text/xml`.

```
AjaxXmlBuilder builder = new AjaxXmlBuilder();
response.setContentType("text/xml");
```

Obtain the catalog entry field values from the `ResultSet` object.

```
String journal=rs.getString("Journal");
String publisher=rs.getString("Publisher");
String edition=rs.getString("Edition");
String title=rs.getString("Title");
String author=rs.getString("Author");
```

Add the field values to the `AjaxXmlBuilder` object.

```
builder.addItem("journal",journal);
builder.addItem("publisher",publisher);
builder.addItem("edition",edition);
builder.addItem("title",title);
builder.addItem("author",author);
```

Output the `AjaxXmlBuilder` XML response using the `toString()` method.

```
out.println(builder.toString());
```

The `FormUpdateServlet` class is listed below.

```
package ajaxtags;

import java.io.*;
import java.sql.*;
import javax.naming.InitialContext;
import javax.servlet.*;
import javax.servlet.http.*;
import org.ajaxtags.helpers.AjaxXmlBuilder;

public class FormUpdateServlet extends HttpServlet {
    public void doGet(HttpServletRequest request,
                      HttpServletResponse response)
throws ServletException, IOException {
        try {
// Obtain value of Catalog Id field to ve validated.
String catalogId = request.getParameter("catalogId");
    if (catalogId.equals("Select Catalog Id")) {
        AjaxXmlBuilder builder = new AjaxXmlBuilder();
        response.setContentType("text/xml");
        response.setHeader("Cache-Control", "no-cache");
        PrintWriter out = response.getWriter();
        builder.addItem("journal", null);
        builder.addItem("publisher", null);
        builder.addItem("edition", null);
        builder.addItem("title", null);
        builder.addItem("author", null);
        out.println(builder.toString());
    }
    if (!(catalogId.equals("Select Catalog Id"))) {
        // Obtain Connection
InitialContext initialContext = new InitialContext();
javax.sql.DataSource ds =
```

```
(javax.sql.DataSource)initialContext.lookup("java:com
p/env/jdbc/AjaxTagsConnectionDS");
java.sql.Connection conn = ds.getConnection();
// Obtain result set
Statement stmt = conn.createStatement();
String query = "SELECT * from Catalog WHERE
CatalogId=" + "'" + catalogId + "'";
ResultSet rs = stmt.executeQuery(query);
// set headers before accessing the Writer
response.setContentType("text/xml");
response.setHeader("Cache-Control", "no-cache");
PrintWriter out = response.getWriter();
// then write the response
// If result set is empty set valid element to true
if (rs.next()) {
AjaxXmlBuilder builder = new AjaxXmlBuilder();
String journal = rs.getString("Journal");
String publisher = rs.getString("Publisher");
String edition = rs.getString("Edition");
String title = rs.getString("Title");
String author = rs.getString("Author");
builder.addItem("journal", journal);
builder.addItem("publisher", publisher);
builder.addItem("edition", edition);
builder.addItem("title", title);
builder.addItem("author", author);
out.println(builder.toString());
} else {
AjaxXmlBuilder builder = new AjaxXmlBuilder();
builder.addItem("journal", null);
builder.addItem("publisher", null);
builder.addItem("edition", null);
builder.addItem("title", null);
builder.addItem("author", null);
out.println(builder.toString());
}
rs.close();
stmt.close();
conn.close();
  }
   } catch (javax.naming.NamingException e) {
    } catch (SQLException e) {
    }
    }
}
```

Copy FormUpdateServlet class to FormUpdateServlet.java class in AjaxTags application in JDeveloper. The *input.jsp* has the input form, the ajax:htmlContent tag to validate input field Catalog Id, and ajax:updateField tag to update form fields for a Catalog Id that already has a catalog entry. JSP *input.jsp* is listed below.

```
<%@ taglib uri="http://ajaxtags.org/tags/ajax"
prefix="ajax"%>
<script type="text/javascript" src="prototype-
1.4.0.js"></script>
<script type="text/javascript"
src="scriptaculous.js"></script>
<script type="text/javascript"
src="overlibmws.js"></script>
<script type="text/javascript"
src="ajaxtags.js"></script>
<html>
 <head>
  <title>AJAXTags</title>
 </head>
 <body><h1>Form for Catalog Entry</h1><form
name="validationForm"
  action="formservlet" method="post">
   <table>
    <tr>
     <td>Catalog Id:</td>
     <td>
      <select id="catalogId" name="catalogId">
       <option value="Select Catalog Id">Select
       Catalog Id</option>
       <option value="catalog1">catalog1</option>
       <option value="catalog2">catalog2</option>
       <option value="catalog3">catalog3</option>
       <option value="catalog4">catalog4</option>
      </select>
     </td>
     <td>
      <div id="validationMessage"></div>
     </td>
    </tr>
    <tr>
     <td>Journal:</td>
     <td>
      <input type="text" size="20" id="journal"
      name="journal"></input>
```

```
    </td>
   </tr>
   <tr>
    <td>Publisher:</td>
    <td>
     <input type="text" size="20" id="publisher"
     name="publisher"></input>
    </td>
   </tr>
   <tr>
    <td>Edition:</td>
    <td>
     <input type="text" size="20" id="edition"
     name="edition"></input>
    </td>
   </tr>
   <tr>
    <td>Title:</td>
    <td>
     <input type="text" size="20" id="title"
     name="title"></input>
    </td>
   </tr>
   <tr>
    <td>Author:</td>
    <td>
     <input type="text" size="20" id="author"
     name="author"></input>
    </td>
   </tr>
   <tr>
    <td>
     <input type="submit" value="Create Catalog
     Entry" id="submitForm"
     name="submitForm"></input>
    </td>
    <td>
     <button id="updateForm">Update Fields</button>
    </td>
   </tr>
  </table>
 </form><ajax:htmlContent baseUrl="formservlet"
source="catalogId"
   target="validationMessage"
parameters="catalogId={catalogId}"/><ajax:updateField
baseUrl="formupdateservlet"
source="catalogId"
```

```
target="journal,publisher,edition,title,author"
action="updateForm"
parser="new ResponseXmlParser()"
parameters="catalogId={catalogId}"/></body>
</html>
```

Copy *input.jsp* listing to the *input.jsp* in AjaxTags application in JDeveloper. When a new catalog entry is created with a valid user id the `FormServlet` servlet redirects the response to *catalog.jsp* if a catalog entry gets created without an error and redirects to *error.jsp* if the catalog entry does not get created and generates an error. In the *catalog.jsp* copy the following scriptlet, which outputs a message to indicate that a catalog entry has been created.

```
<%out.println("Catalog Entry Created");%>
```

To the *error.jsp* copy the following scriptlet, which outputs a message to indicate that an error was generated in creating the catalog entry.

```
<%out.println("Error in creating Catalog Entry");%>
```

Next, we shall run the AjaxTags application in OC4J server. Right-click on the *input.jsp* and select **Run** as shown in Fig. 6.7.

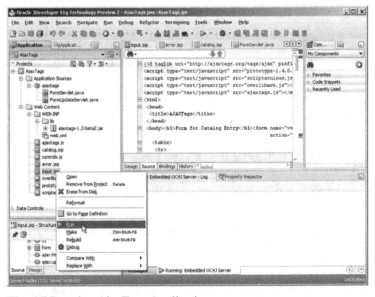

Fig. 6.7 Running AjaxTags Application

Select a Catalog Id value from the selection list as shown in Fig. 6.8.

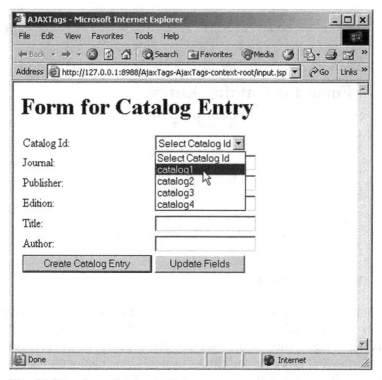

Fig. 6.8 Selecting a Catalog Id Value

An Ajax request gets sent to the server with the `ajax:htmlContent` AjaxTags tag. The server returns an HTML response about the validity of the Catalog Id value. As the `catalog1` value is already in the database, a validation message gets displayed, "Catalog Id is not Valid" as shown in Fig. 6.9.

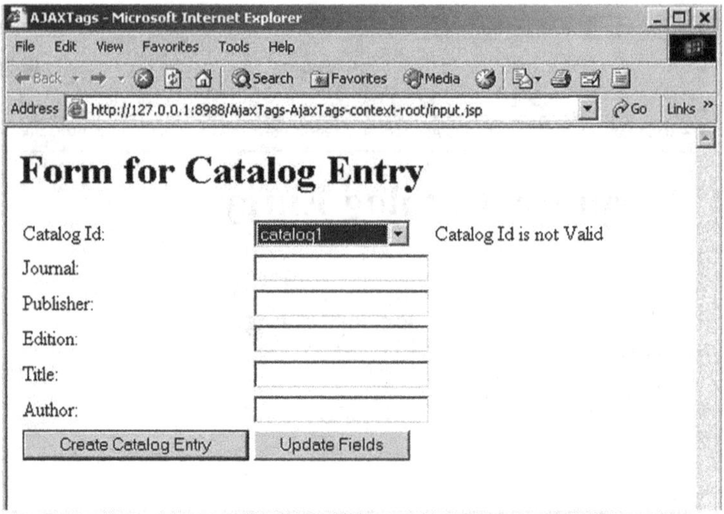

Fig. 6.9 Validating Catalog Id

Update the form fields with the **Update Fields** button. The **Update Fields** button sends an Ajax request with the `ajax:updateField` AjaxTags tag. The XML server response gets parsed by the `ResponseXmlParser` and the form fields get filled with the response values as shown in Fig. 6.10.

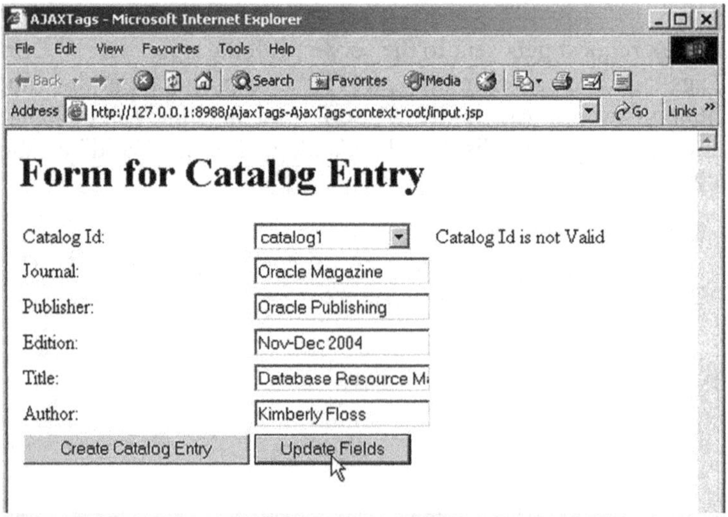

Fig. 6.10 Updating Form Fields

To create a new catalog entry, select a Catalog Id value, `Catalog4` for example, that is not already in the database. A validation message gets displayed, "Catalog Id is Valid". Click on the `Update Fields` button. As the `catalog4` Catalog Id is not in the database, `null` values get specified as shown in Fig. 6.11.

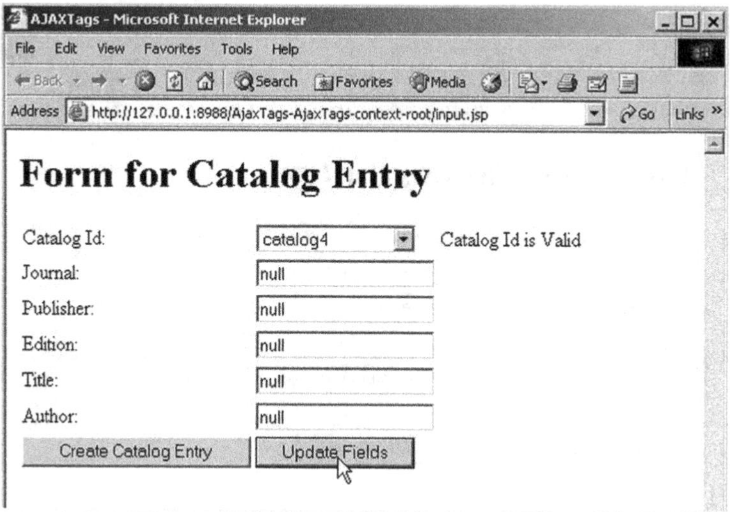

Fig. 6.11 Valid Catalog Id

Specify field values for a new catalog entry with Catalog Id `catalog4` Click on the Create Catalog button to create a catalog entry as shown in Fig. 6.12.

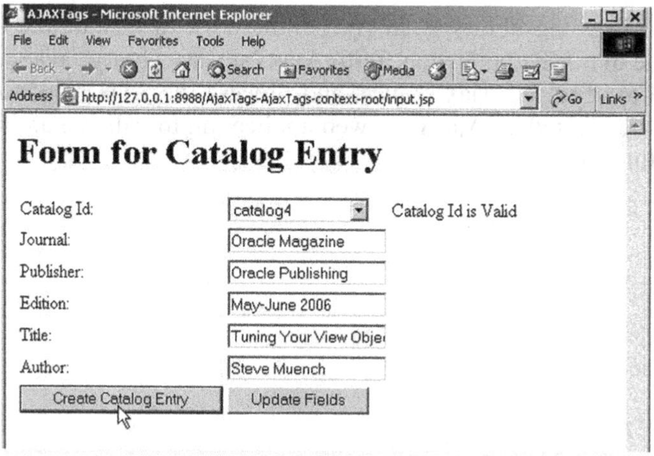

Fig. 6.12 Creating a Catalog Entry

A new catalog entry gets created in the database. If the *input.jsp* is re-run and the `catalog4` value is re-selected a validation message gets displayed, "Catalog Id is not Valid". Update the form fields with the **Update Fields** button as shown in Fig. 6.13. The form gets filled with the catalog entry previously created.

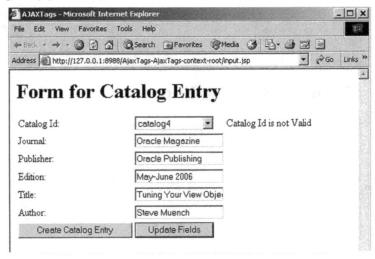

Fig. 6.13 Reselecting a Catalog Id

6.6 Summary

The AjaxTags tag library is an Ajax framework to include the Ajax web technique in a JSP application. With AjaxTags tag library JavaScript is not required to send the Ajax request and process the Ajax response. In this chapter we created an AjaxTags web application to validate an input form for creating a catalog entry.

7 Ajax with JSF-Ajax4jsf

7.1 Introduction

JavaServer Faces (JSF) provides a set of components to develop user interfaces (UIs) for J2EE applications. We have used HTML components in the previous chapters. Ajax may also be used with JSF UI components using JBoss Ajax4jsf. Ajax4jsf is an open source framework that adds Ajax functionality to JSF applications without requiring any JavaScript. JDeveloper provides a Component Palette for JSF Core and JSF HTML components from which components may be added to a JSF page. In this chapter we shall create an input form for a catalog entry using JSF Components provided in JDeveloper and add Ajax to the input form using Ajax4jsf.

7.2 Overview of Ajax4jsf

Ajax4jsf provides a component library that may be used in a JSF page for page-wide Ajax functionality. Ajax4jsf supports action and value change listeners, and server-side validation and conversion facilities of the JSF framework. Ajax4jsf also supports management of static and dynamic resources such as images, and CSS stylesheets. Ajax4jsf also supports the Facelets framework. To use Ajax4jsf, one would need the following: JDK 1.4-1.6, JSF 1.1 or 1.2, a J2EE application server such as WebSphere 5.1-6 or WebLogic 8.1-9.0 or OC4J 10.1.3, and browser that supports XMLHttpRequest such as Internet Explorer 6+ or Netscape Navigator 6+. An event on the page invokes an Ajax request and specified regions of the page are updated with the Ajax response. Next, we shall discuss some of the elements of the Ajax4jsf framework.

7.2.1 Ajax Filter

The Ajax filter is registered in the `web.xml` file and distinguishes between a JSF request and an Ajax request. In a JSF request the complete JSF page is synchronized with the JSF component tree. While in an Ajax request only the Ajax region, specified by `<a4j:region>` is updated with the Ajax response.

7.2.2 Ajax Action Components

These are the components that are used to send an Ajax request from the browser to the server. Ajax action components are: `AjaxCommandButton`, `AjaxCommandLink`, and `AjaxSupport`.

7.2.3 Ajax Containers

An Ajax container is an area on a JSF page that is to be decoded during an Ajax request and updated with the Ajax response.

7.2.4 JavaScript Engine

The JavaScript engine runs on the client-side and updates the different regions of a JSF page with the Ajax response.

7.2.5 Ajax4jsf Component Library

Ajax4jsf provides a component library to implement Ajax functionality in JSF. Some of the commonly used components are discussed in Table 7.1.

Table 7.1 Ajax4jsf Components

Component	Description	Attributes
<a4j:region>	Specifies an area that is decoded in an Ajax request. However, components out of the region may be updated. The region defined by f:view is the default region.	renderRegionOnly-If set to true (default), only the region is updated with the response. rendered-If set to false the component is not rendered. binding-Component binding. ajaxListener-Binding to a public method that returns void and accepts an AjaxEvent.

Table 7.1 (continued)

Component	Description	Attributes
<a4j:poll>	Sends periodical Ajax requests at specified frequency (ms) and updates the page with the response.	interval-Specifies interval (ms) after which an Ajax request is sent. Default value is 1000 ms (1 sec). actionListener, action,oncomplete,reRender,binding-Same as for a4j:support.
<a4j:commandLink>	Provides a link that submits a form with Ajax.	reRender-Specifies component Ids that are updated with Ajax response. actionListener,oncomplete, action,requestDelay,binding-Same as for a4j:support.
<a4j:commandButton>	Provides a command button to submit a form with Ajax.	reRender,actionListener, oncomplete,action,requestDelay, binding-Same as for a4j:commandLink.
<a4j:support>	Adds Ajax support to a JSF component. This component generates an Ajax request on a specified event.	actionListener-Specifies method binding for a public method that returns void and accepts an ActionEvent. action-Specifies a method binding for a backing bean method that is invoked after the specified event and before components are re-rendered with the Ajax response. oncomplete-JavaScript code to invoke after an Ajax request completes. reRender-Specifies a comma separated list of component Ids that are updated with the Ajax response. requestDelay-Specifies number of seconds delay (ms) to send an Ajax request. event-JavaScript event that initiates an Ajax request. binding-Component binding.

Table 7.1 (continued)

Component	Description	Attributes
<a4j:outputPanel>	Provides component grouping in the output area that is updated with Ajax response. The page area specified by this component may be updated in addition to the components specified in reRender attribute of a component that initiates an Ajax request.	layout-Specifies HTML layout for generated markup. A value of "block" generates a <div> element. A value of "inline" generates a <span> element. style-Specifies CSS stylesheet. ajaxRendered-Specifies if the component is to be updated in addition to the components updated with reRender.
<a4j:mediaOutput>	Generates multi-media output.	mimeType-Mime-type of generated content, for example, image/jpeg.
<a4j:form>	Provides a form that submits with Ajax.	reRender,oncomplete,requestDelay,binding

7.3 Setting the Environment

We shall develop a form validation application using JSF UI components and Ajax4jsf. The form shall be used to create catalog entries in a database table; a catalog entry has a unique field, catalog ID, and consists of columns journal, publisher, edition, title, author. The Ajax web technique is used to dynamically validate a catalog ID. Without Ajax the complete form has to be posted to the server to check if a catalog ID is valid. If the specified catalog ID is already in the database, the form has to be re-submitted with another catalog ID. With Ajax a catalog ID may be dynamically validated as the value is specified in the catalog entry form. Catalog entries shall be stored in Oracle database, therefore, first we install Oracle Database 10g, including sample schemas, and create a database instance ORCL. Create a database table with SQL script in following listing.

```
CREATE TABLE OE.Catalog(CatalogID VARCHAR(25)
PRIMARY KEY, Journal VARCHAR(25), Publisher
VARCHAR(25),
  Edition VARCHAR(25), Title Varchar(255), Author
Varchar(25));

INSERT INTO OE.Catalog VALUES('catalog1', 'Oracle
Magazine', 'Oracle Publishing', 'July-August 2006',
'Evolving Grid Management', 'David Baum');

INSERT INTO OE.Catalog VALUES('catalog2', 'Oracle
Magazine', 'Oracle Publishing', 'July-August
2005','Tuning Undo Tablespace', 'Kimberly Floss');
```

Install JDeveloper 11g, which supports JSF 1.1. Download the Ajax4jsf binary distribution[1] zip file, jboss-ajax4jsf-1.1.0.zip. Extract the zip file to a directory.

7.4 Creating an Ajax4jsf Application

In this section we shall create a JSF application and add Ajax functionality to it with Ajax4jsf. The JSF application consists of an input form for a catalog entry. The form consists of field Catalog ID, Journal, Publisher, Edition, Title, and Author. The form requires a unique Catalog ID, which is dynamically validated on the server and a message displayed to indicate the validity of the Catalog ID. First, create a JDeveloper application with **File>New**. Select **General** in the **Categories** and **Application** in the **Items** in **New Gallery** window. Click on **OK**. In the **Create Application** window specify an application name and click on **OK**. In the **Create Project** window specify a project name and click on **OK**. An application and a project get added to the **Application-Navigator**. Next, create a JSF page. Select **File>New** and select **Web Tier>JSF** in **Categories** in the **New Gallery** window. Select **JSF Page** in **Items** and click on **OK** as shown in Fig. 7.1.

---

[1] Download Ajax4jsf- http://labs.jboss.com/jbossajax4jsf/

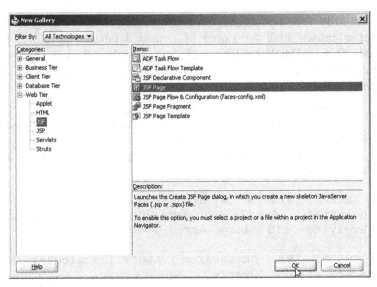

Fig. 7.1 Selecting JSF Page

In the **Create JSF Page** window specify a **File Name**, *input.jsp*, and in **Page Implementation** select **Automatically Expose UI Components in a new Managed Bean** and click on **OK** as shown in Fig. 7.2.

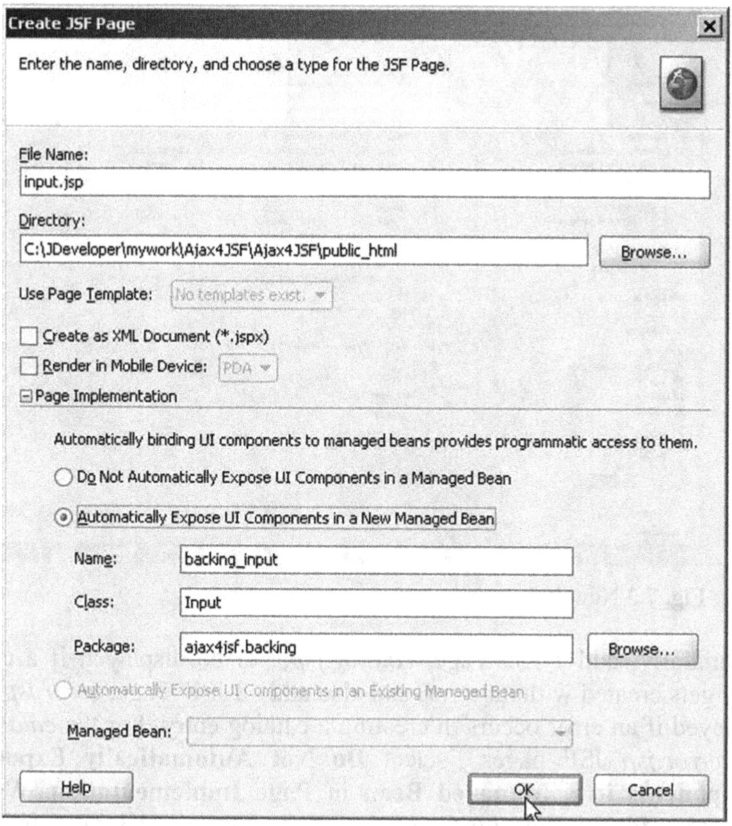

Fig. 7.2 Creating a JSF Page

A JSF page gets created and `taglib` declarations for the JSF Core 1.0 and JSF HTML 1.0 libraries get added to the JSF page by default as shown in Fig. 7.3.

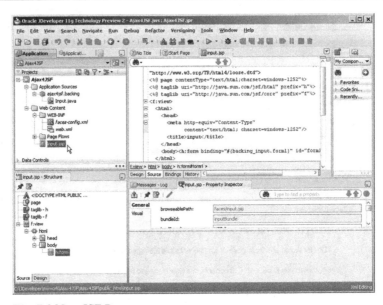

Fig. 7.3 New JSF Page

Similarly, add a JSF Page, *catalog.jsp*, to be displayed if a catalog entry gets created without error, and also add a JSF Page, *error.jsp*, to be displayed if an error occurs in creating a catalog entry. For the *catalog.jsp* and *error.jsp* JSF pages select **Do Not Automatically Expose UI Components in a Managed Bean** in **Page Implementation**. We also need to add the *lib/Ajax4jsf.jar* and *lib/oscache-2.3.2.jar* from the Ajax4jsf binary distribution to the project. To add a library to Ajax4jsf project select **Tools>Project Properties**. In the **Project Properties** window select **Libraries** and add a JAR file with **Add Jar/Directory**. Also add libraries Commons Beanutils 1.6.1, Commons Collections 2.1, Commons Logging 1.0.3, and Commons Digester 1.5 with **Add Library**. The project libraries for the Ajax4jsf project are shown in Fig. 7.4.

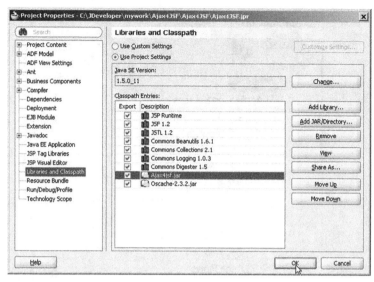

Fig. 7.4 Ajax4jsf Application Libraries

Copy the JAR files, *ajax4jsf.jar* and *oscache-2.3.2.jar*, from the *lib* directory of the Ajax4jsf binary distribution to the *WEB-INF/lib* directory of the Ajax4jsf application. The directory structure of the Ajax4jsf application is shown in Fig. 7.5.

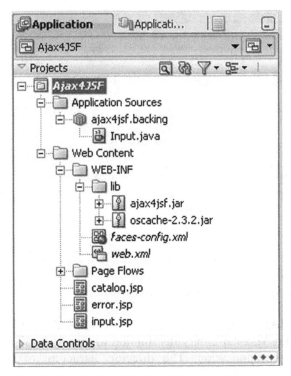

Fig. 7.5 Ajax4jsf Application Directory Structure

Next, we shall create an input form for a catalog entry using JSF components. First, add a **Panel Grid** component to the *input.jsp* page from the **JSF HTML** component library as shown in Fig. 7.6.

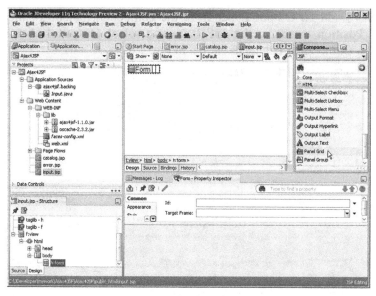

Fig. 7.6 Adding a JSF PanelGrid

In the **Create PanelGrid Wizard** click on **Next**. In the **PanelGrid Options** window select **Create empty panel grid** and specify number of columns as 2 as shown in Fig. 7.7. Click on **Finish**. The components added to the panel grid shall get arranged in 2 columns.

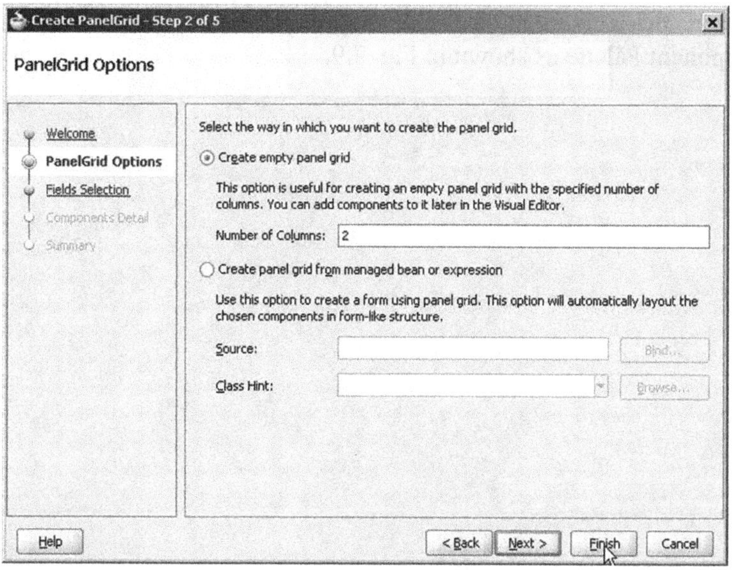

Fig. 7.7 Specifying Number of Columns in PanelGrid

Next, add an Output Label from the component palette to the panel grid. Position cursor in the JSF Page and select **Output Label** in JSF HTML Component Palette as shown in Fig. 7.8.

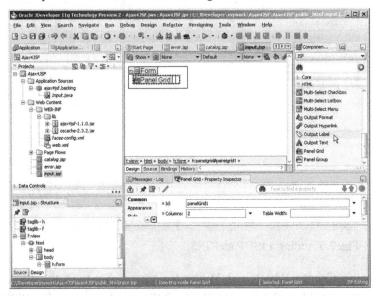

Fig. 7.8 Adding an Output Label

Add an Input Text from the component palette to the panel grid. Position the cursor in the JSF Page and select **Input Text** in the Component Palette as shown in Fig. 7.9.

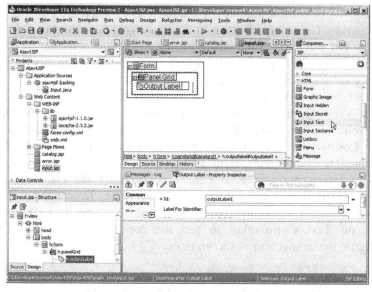

Fig. 7.9 Adding an Input Text

An Input Text gets added to the panel grid as shown in Fig. 7.10.

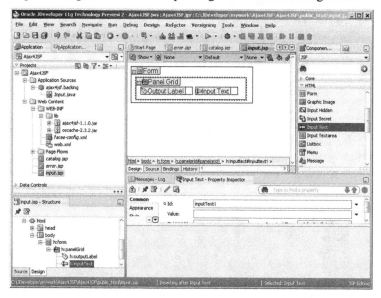

Fig. 7.10 Creating a Panel Grid

Similarly, add 5 more sets of **Output Label**s and **Input Text**s to the Panel Grid. The Output Labels and Input Texts get added to 2 columns, because we specified number of columns as 2 when creating the Panel Grid. Add a **Command Button** to the panel grid for submitting the form. Add an **Output Text** to the panel grid for displaying a validation message indicating the validity of a Catalog ID value. In the **Property Inspector** specify values for the output labels and the command button.

Next, we need to create a JDBC connection with the Oracle database. Select **View>Database Navigator** to display the **Database Navigator**. Right-click on the Ajax4jsf node in the Databases Navigator and select **New Connection**. In the **Create Database Connection** window specify a **Connection Name** and select **Connection Type** as **Oracle (JDBC)**. Specify **Username** as **OE** and the **Password** for the **OE** user. In the **Oracle (JDBC) Settings** window select the thin **Driver**. Specify **Host Name** as localhost and **JDBC Port** as 1521. Specify **SID** as ORCL. Click on **Test Connection** to test the connection. Click on **OK** to configure the connection as shown in Fig. 7.11.

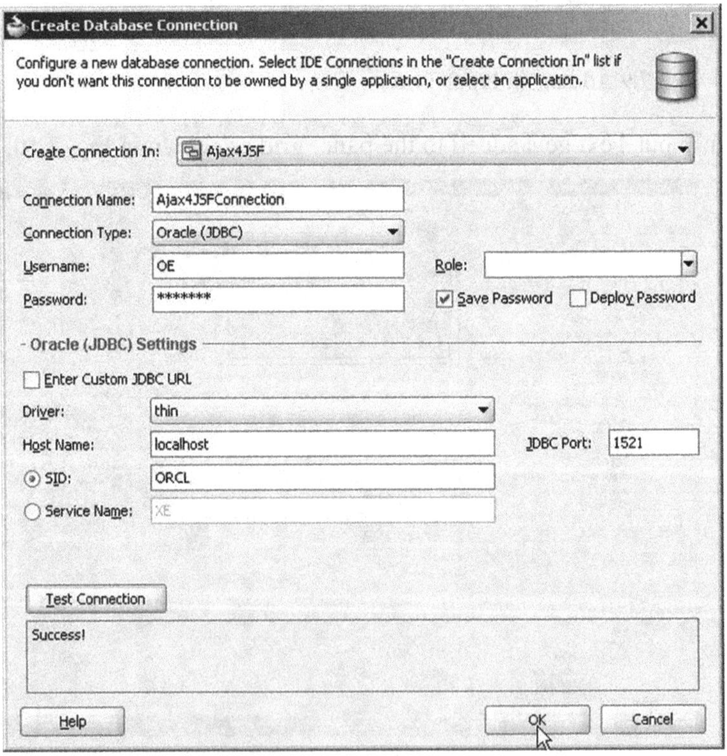

Fig. 7.11 Creating a JDBC Connection

A connection gets added to the **Database Navigator** as shown in Fig. 7.12.

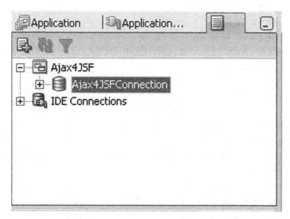

Fig. 7.12 JDBC Connection for Ajax4jsf Application

To the web.xml file add a resource-ref element for the Oracle datasource. Add an ajax4jsf filter and filter mapping to web.xml. Also specify a listener class. The web.xml file is shown in following listing.

```
<?xml version = '1.0' encoding = 'windows-1252'?>
<web-app
xmlns:xsi="http://www.w3.org/2001/XMLSchema-instance"
  xsi:schemaLocation="http://java.sun.com/xml/ns/j2ee
http://java.sun.com/xml/ns/j2ee/web-app_2_4.xsd"
           version="2.4"
xmlns="http://java.sun.com/xml/ns/j2ee">
<description>Empty     web.xml     file     for     Web
Application</description>
  <context-param>
  <param-name>javax.faces.STATE_SAVING_METHOD</param-
  name>
     <param-value>server</param-value>
     </context-param>
     <filter>
        <display-name>Ajax4jsf Filter</display-name>
         <filter-name>ajax4jsf</filter-name>
     <filter-class>org.ajax4jsf.Filter</filter-class>
     </filter>
     <filter-mapping>
         <filter-name>ajax4jsf</filter-name>
         <servlet-name>Faces Servlet</servlet-name>
         <dispatcher>REQUEST</dispatcher>
```

```
        <dispatcher>FORWARD</dispatcher>
        <dispatcher>INCLUDE</dispatcher>
    </filter-mapping>
    <listener>
 <listener-
 class>com.sun.faces.config.ConfigureListener</list
 ener-class>
 </listener>
    <servlet>
        <servlet-name>Faces Servlet</servlet-name>
        <servlet-class>javax.faces.webapp.FacesServlet
    </servlet-class>
        <load-on-startup>1</load-on-startup>
    </servlet>
    <servlet-mapping>
    <servlet-name>Faces Servlet</servlet-name>
    <url-pattern>/faces/*</url-pattern>
    </servlet-mapping>
    <session-config>
    <session-timeout>35</session-timeout>
    </session-config>
    <mime-mapping>
        <extension>html</extension>
        <mime-type>text/html</mime-type>
    </mime-mapping>
    <mime-mapping>
        <extension>txt</extension>
        <mime-type>text/plain</mime-type>
    </mime-mapping>
    <resource-ref>
    <res-ref-name>jdbc/Ajax4JSFConnectionDS</res-
    ref-name>
        <res-type>javax.sql.DataSource</res-type>
        <res-auth>Container</res-auth>
    </resource-ref>
</web-app>
```

Modify faces-config.xml. Add a navigation-rule for navigating to the *catalog.jsp* page if a catalog entry gets created and navigating to the *error.jsp* page if an error is generated in updating the catalog database table. JSF configuration file, *faces-config.xml* is shown in following listing.

```
<?xml version="1.0" encoding="windows-1252"?>
<!DOCTYPE faces-config PUBLIC
    "-//Sun Microsystems, Inc.//DTD JavaServer Faces
Config 1.1//EN"
```

```
 "http://java.sun.com/dtd/web-
facesconfig_1_1.dtd">
  <faces-config
xmlns="http://java.sun.com/JSF/Configuration">
    <managed-bean>
<managed-bean-name>backing_input</managed-bean-name>
<managed-bean-class>ajaxjsf.backing.Input</managed-
bean-class>
  <managed-bean-scope>request</managed-bean-scope>
  <!--oracle-jdev-comment:managed-bean-jsp-
link:1input.jsp-->
    </managed-bean>
    <navigation-rule>
    <from-view-id>/input.jsp</from-view-id>
    <navigation-case>
    <from-outcome>catalog</from-outcome>
    <to-view-id>/catalog.jsp</to-view-id>
    </navigation-case>
    <navigation-case>
    <from-outcome>error</from-outcome>
    <to-view-id>/error.jsp</to-view-id>
    </navigation-case>
    </navigation-rule>
  </faces-config>
```

7.5 Sending an Ajax Request

In this section we shall send an Ajax request from the JSF page, *input.jsp* using Ajax4jsf. Add a `<a4j:support/>` element to the Catalog ID input text field. Specify the event that initiates an Ajax request using the `event` attribute. Specify a backing bean method, `inputText_action`, to invoke using the `action` attribute when an Ajax request is sent. Specify the components to be updated with the Ajax response using the `reRender` attribute. The `h:inputText` element for the Catalog ID input field is as follows.

```
<h:inputText binding="#{backing_input.inputText1}"
  id="inputText1">
  <a4j:support                          event="onkeyup"
action="#{backing_input.inputText_action}"
  reRender="inputText2,inputText3,inputText4,inputTex
t5,inputText6,commandButton1,outputText1" />
  </h:inputText>
```

To use the Ajax4jsf component library, add the following `taglib` directive to the JSF page *input.jsp*.

```
<%@ taglib uri=https://ajax4jsf.dev.java.net/ajax
prefix="a4j"%>
```

Create a catalog entry when the form is submitted with the command button. Add an `action` attribute to the command button to invoke the `commandButton_action` method when the command button is clicked. The command button element is as follows.

```
<h:commandButton value="Submit"
  binding="#{backing_input.commandButton1}"
action="#{backing_input.commandButton_action}"
  id="commandButton1"/>
```

JSF page *input.jsp* is listed below.

```
<%@ taglib uri="https://ajax4jsf.dev.java.net/ajax"
prefix="a4j"%>
  <%@ taglib uri="http://java.sun.com/jsf/html"
prefix="h"%>
  <%@ taglib uri="http://java.sun.com/jsf/core"
prefix="f"%>
  <f:view>
    <html>
      <head>
        <meta http-equiv="Content-Type"
         content="text/html; charset=windows-1252"/>
        <title>input</title>
  <h3>Catalog Entry Form</h3>
      </head>
          <body><h:form
          binding="#{backing_input.form1}"
          id="form1">
        <h:panelGrid                      columns="2"
  binding="#{backing_input.panelGrid1}"
                    id="panelGrid1">
            <h:outputLabel value="Catalog ID"
    binding="#{backing_input.outputLabel1}"
            id="outputLabel1"/>
  <h:inputText binding="#{backing_input.inputText1}"
            id="inputText1">
  <a4j:support                      event="onkeyup"
action="#{backing_input.inputText_action}"
  reRender="inputText2,inputText3,inputText4,inputTex
t5,inputText6,commandButton1,outputText1" />
```

```
      </h:inputText><h:outputLabel            value="Journal"
binding="#{backing_input.outputLabel2}"
   id="outputLabel2"/>
               <h:inputText
binding="#{backing_input.inputText2}"
id="inputText2"/>
   <h:outputLabel value="Publisher"
   binding="#{backing_input.outputLabel3}"
   id="outputLabel3"/>
   <h:inputText   binding="#{backing_input.inputText3}"
id="inputText3"/>
   <h:outputLabel                          value="Edition"
binding="#{backing_input.outputLabel4}"
   id="outputLabel4"/>
   <h:inputText   binding="#{backing_input.inputText4}"
id="inputText4"/>
               <h:outputLabel            value="Title"
binding="#{backing_input.outputLabel5}"
   id="outputLabel5"/>
   <h:inputText   binding="#{backing_input.inputText5}"
id="inputText5"/>
               <h:outputLabel            value="Author"
binding="#{backing_input.outputLabel6}"
   id="outputLabel6"/>
    <h:inputText  binding="#{backing_input.inputText6}"
id="inputText6"/>
   <h:commandButton value="Submit"
   binding="#{backing_input.commandButton1}"
action="#{backing_input.commandButton_action}"
   id="commandButton1"/>
   <h:outputText
binding="#{backing_input.outputText1}"
   id="outputText1"/>
               </h:panelGrid>
         </h:form></body>
      </html>
   </f:view>
   <%-- oracle-jdev-comment:auto-binding-backing-bean-
name:backing_input--%>
```

Modify *catalog.jsp* to output a message that a catalog entry has been created and modify *error.jsp* to output a message that an error has been generated in updating the database.

7.6 Processing an Ajax Request

On the server-side the Catalog ID field value is validated with the database table Catalog. If the Catalog ID value is already specified in the database a validation message, "Catalog Id is not valid" gets displayed in the input form. If the Catalog ID value is not already specified in the database, a validation message, "Catalog ID is valid" gets displayed in the input form. We have used the business logic that if a catalog id is not already defined the catalog id is valid. Additional business logic may be added to check if the catalog id matches a pattern specified in a regular expression. The `inputText_action` method gets invoked when a value is specified in the Catalog ID input field. An Ajax request is sent with each modification in the Catalog ID input field. In the `inputText_action` method obtain a connection with the Oracle database using the Oracle datasource configured in JDeveloper.

```
InitialContext initialContext = new InitialContext();
javax.sql.DataSource ds =
(javax.sql.DataSource)initialContext.lookup("java:com
p/env/jdbc/OracleDBConnectionDS");
java.sql.Connection connection = ds.getConnection();
```

Create a `Statement` object with a scrollable result set type to run an SQL statement.

```
Statement stmt =
connection.createStatement(ResultSet.TYPE_SCROLL_INSE
NSITIVE,
ResultSet.CONCUR_READ_ONLY);
```

Obtain the Catalog ID value specified in the input form and create a SQL query to run in the Oracle database.

```
String catalogID = (String)inputText1.getValue();
String query =
        "SELECT * from Catalog WHERE CATALOGID=" +
"'" + catalogID + "'";
```

Run the SQL query and obtain a result set.

```
rs = stmt.executeQuery(query);
```

If the result set is not empty, set the validation message to "Catalog Id is not valid.", set the field values, and disable the command button.

```
if (rs.next()) {
    inputText2.setValue(rs.getString(2));
    inputText3.setValue(rs.getString(3));
    inputText4.setValue(rs.getString(4));
    inputText5.setValue(rs.getString(5));
    inputText6.setValue(rs.getString(6));
      outputText1.setValue(new String("Catalog  Id  is
      not Valid"));
    commandButton1.setDisabled(true);
}
```

If the result set is empty, implying that the Catalog ID specified in the input form is not already in the database, set the validation message to, "Catalog Id is valid.", set the field values to empty Strings and enable the **Submit** button.

```
else {
    inputText2.setValue(new String());
    inputText3.setValue(new String());
    inputText4.setValue(new String());
    inputText5.setValue(new String());
    inputText6.setValue(new String());
    outputText1.setValue(new  String("Catalog  Id  is
    Valid"));
    commandButton1.setDisabled(false);
}
```

If the Catalog ID is valid, retrieve the form field values, obtain a connection with the database and create a new catalog entry. The backing bean class, *Input.java* is listed below.

```
package ajax4jsf.backing;

import java.sql.*;
import
javax.faces.component.html.HtmlCommandButton;
import javax.faces.component.html.HtmlForm;
import javax.faces.component.html.HtmlInputText;
import javax.faces.component.html.HtmlOutputLabel;
import javax.faces.component.html.HtmlOutputText;
import javax.faces.component.html.HtmlPanelGrid;
import javax.naming.InitialContext;

public class Input {
    private HtmlForm form1;
    private HtmlPanelGrid panelGrid1;
    private HtmlOutputLabel outputLabel1;
    private HtmlInputText inputText1;
```

```java
    private HtmlOutputLabel outputLabel2;
    private HtmlInputText inputText2;
    private HtmlOutputLabel outputLabel3;
    private HtmlInputText inputText3;
    private HtmlOutputLabel outputLabel4;
    private HtmlInputText inputText4;
    private HtmlOutputLabel outputLabel5;
    private HtmlInputText inputText5;
    private HtmlOutputLabel outputLabel6;
    private HtmlInputText inputText6;
    private HtmlCommandButton commandButton1;
    private HtmlOutputText outputText1;
public void setForm1(HtmlForm form1) {
        this.form1 = form1;
    }
public HtmlForm getForm1() {
        return form1;
    }
 public       void       setPanelGrid1(HtmlPanelGrid
  panelGrid1) {
        this.panelGrid1 = panelGrid1;
    }
public HtmlPanelGrid getPanelGrid1() {
        return panelGrid1;
    }
public     void     setOutputLabel1(HtmlOutputLabel
outputLabel1) {
        this.outputLabel1 = outputLabel1;
    }
public HtmlOutputLabel getOutputLabel1() {
        return outputLabel1;
    }
public void setInputText1(HtmlInputText inputText1)
{
        this.inputText1 = inputText1;
    }
public HtmlInputText getInputText1() {
        return inputText1;
    }
public     void     setOutputLabel2(HtmlOutputLabel
outputLabel2) {
        this.outputLabel2 = outputLabel2;
    }
public HtmlOutputLabel getOutputLabel2() {
        return outputLabel2;
    }
```

```java
public void setInputText2(HtmlInputText inputText2)
{
      this.inputText2 = inputText2;
   }
 public HtmlInputText getInputText2() {
      return inputText2;
   }
public     void       setOutputLabel3(HtmlOutputLabel
outputLabel3) {
      this.outputLabel3 = outputLabel3;
   }
  public HtmlOutputLabel getOutputLabel3() {
      return outputLabel3;
   }
public        void        setInputText3(HtmlInputText
inputText3) {
      this.inputText3 = inputText3;
   }
   public HtmlInputText getInputText3() {
      return inputText3;
   }
public     void       setOutputLabel4(HtmlOutputLabel
outputLabel4) {
      this.outputLabel4 = outputLabel4;
   }
public HtmlOutputLabel getOutputLabel4() {
      return outputLabel4;
   }
public         void        setInputText4(HtmlInputText
inputText4) {
      this.inputText4 = inputText4;
   }
public HtmlInputText getInputText4() {
      return inputText4;
   }
   public     void      setOutputLabel5(HtmlOutputLabel
   outputLabel5) {
      this.outputLabel5 = outputLabel5;
   }
public HtmlOutputLabel getOutputLabel5() {
      return outputLabel5;
   }
public         void        setInputText5(HtmlInputText
inputText5) {
      this.inputText5 = inputText5;
   }
  public HtmlInputText getInputText5() {
```

```
                return inputText5;
        }
    public     void      setOutputLabel6(HtmlOutputLabel
    outputLabel6) {
            this.outputLabel6 = outputLabel6;
        }
     public HtmlOutputLabel getOutputLabel6() {
            return outputLabel6;
        }
    public       void       setInputText6(HtmlInputText
    inputText6) {
            this.inputText6 = inputText6;
        }
    public HtmlInputText getInputText6() {
            return inputText6;
        }
    public    void   setCommandButton1(HtmlCommandButton
    commandButton1) {
            this.commandButton1 = commandButton1;
        }
    public HtmlCommandButton getCommandButton1() {
            return commandButton1;
        }
    public      void       setOutputText1(HtmlOutputText
    outputText1) {
            this.outputText1 = outputText1;
        }
    public HtmlOutputText getOutputText1() {
            return outputText1;
        }
    public String inputText_action() {
            ResultSet rs = null;
            try {
                    InitialContext initialContext = new
        InitialContext();
        javax.sql.DataSource ds =
      (javax.sql.DataSource)initialContext.lookup("java:c
    omp/env/jdbc/Ajax4JSFConnectionDS");
                    java.sql.Connection    connection    =
    ds.getConnection();
        Statement stmt =
      connection.createStatement(ResultSet.TYPE_SCROLL_IN
      SENSITIVE,
      ResultSet.CONCUR_READ_ONLY);
      String catalogID = (String)inputText1.getValue();
      String query =
```

```
   "SELECT * from Catalog WHERE CATALOGID=" + "'" +
   catalogID +
                     "'";
      rs = stmt.executeQuery(query);
      if (rs.next()) {
inputText2.setValue(rs.getString(2));
inputText3.setValue(rs.getString(3));
inputText4.setValue(rs.getString(4));
inputText5.setValue(rs.getString(5));
inputText6.setValue(rs.getString(6));
outputText1.setValue(new String("Catalog Id is not
Valid"));
commandButton1.setDisabled(true);
   } else {
      inputText2.setValue(new String());
      inputText3.setValue(new String());
      inputText4.setValue(new String());
      inputText5.setValue(new String());
      inputText6.setValue(new String());
      outputText1.setValue(new String("Catalog Id is
   Valid"));
      commandButton1.setDisabled(false);
   }
            } catch (SQLException e) {
                System.out.println(e.getMessage());
            } catch (javax.naming.NamingException e) {
                System.out.println(e.getMessage());
            }
            return null;
        }
        public String commandButton_action() {
            try {
                //Obtain Connection
                InitialContext initialContext = new
    InitialContext();
                javax.sql.DataSource ds =
(javax.sql.DataSource)initialContext.lookup("java:com
p/env/jdbc/Ajax4JSFConnectionDS");
                java.sql.Connection conn =
    ds.getConnection();
   String catalogId = (String)inputText1.getValue();
   String journal = (String)inputText2.getValue();
   String publisher = (String)inputText3.getValue();
   String edition = (String)inputText4.getValue();
   String title = (String)inputText5.getValue();
   String author = (String)inputText6.getValue();
```

```
Statement stmt = conn.createStatement();
String sql =
"INSERT INTO Catalog VALUES(" + "\'" + catalogId +
"\'" + "," +
                    "\'" + journal + "\'" + "," + "\'"
+ publisher + "\'" + "," +
                    "\'" + edition + "\'" + "," + "\'"
+ title + "\'" + "," +
                    "\'" + author + "\'" + ")";
stmt.execute(sql);
stmt.close();
conn.close();
} catch (javax.naming.NamingException e) {
            return "error";
} catch (SQLException e) {
            return "error";
}
        return "catalog";
    }
}
```

7.7 Processing the Ajax Response

In this section we shall validate the Catalog ID value specified in the input form with Oracle database table Catalog. If the Catalog ID is not valid, a message shall be displayed to indicate that the Catalog ID is not valid, the form field values shall get filled, and the **Submit** button shall get disabled. If the Catalog ID is valid, a validation message shall indicate the same, the form fields shall be set to empty String values and the **Submit** button shall be enabled. For a valid Catalog ID, we shall create a catalog entry with the **Submit** button. The JSF components set in the reRender attribute of the a4j:support tag specify the components to be updated with the Ajax response. Next, run the JSF page. Right-click on *input.jsp* and select **Run** as shown in Fig. 7.13.

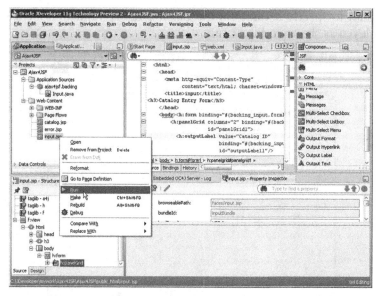

Fig. 7.13 Running Ajax4jsf Application

The catalog entry form gets displayed as shown in Fig. 7.14.

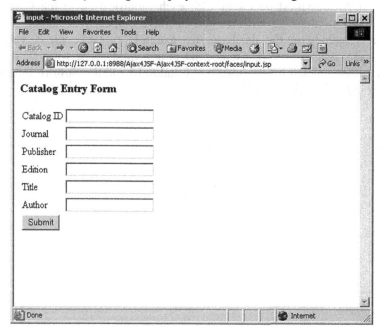

Fig. 7.14 Catalog Entry Form

Start to specify a value for the Catalog ID. A validation message gets displayed as shown in Fig. 7.15.

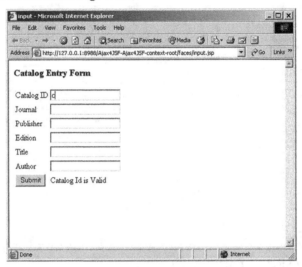

Fig. 7.15 Validating Catalog ID

An Ajax request gets sent with each modification to the Catalog ID field and a validation message gets displayed. Specify a Catalog ID value that is already in the database, for example `catalog2`. A validation message gets displayed:"Catalog ID is not valid". The form field values get autocompleted for the specified Catalog Id and the **Submit** button gets disabled as shown in Fig. 7.16.

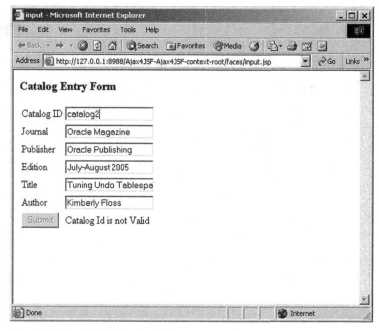

Fig. 7.16 Non Valid Catalog ID

To create a catalog entry, specify a Catalog ID value that is valid. Specify the form field values and click on **Submit** button as shown in Fig. 7.17. A catalog entry gets created.

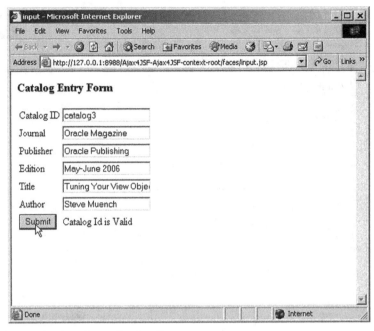

Fig. 7.17 Creating a Catalog Entry

7.8 Summary

The Ajax4jsf component library adds Ajax functionality to JSF applications. Thus the set of UI components provided by JSF may be availed of in combination with Ajax. In this chapter we used the Ajax4jsf framework to send an Ajax request from a input form to validate catalog id for a catalog entry. If the catalog id is already defined the input form gets auto-completed with the catalog entry values in the Ajax response. If the catalog id is not already defined a new catalog entry may be created.

8 Ajax with PHP-Xajax

8.1 Introduction

According to Ajaxian.com[1] on Ajax PHP is the most commonly used Platform for Ajax. PHP may be used on the server side by specifying a PHP file as the URL in the open() method of the XMLHttpRequest object. PHP may also be used with Ajax with a PHP framework for Ajax. Various PHP Ajax frameworks are available. According to the survey by Ajaxian.com, Xajax is the most commonly used PHP Ajax framework. Xajax is an open source, object oriented, PHP class library, with which, PHP scripts may be used for server side processing. In this chapter we shall create a Xajax application.

Xajax is used to communicate asynchronously between a client application and a server side application comprised of PHP scripts. Xajax generates JavaScript wrapper functions for PHP functions on the server side that may be accessed from a client application. When a client application invokes the wrapper functions, an XMLHttpRequest object is initiated and an XMLHttpRequest object is sent to the server. On the server, the XJAX object receives the XMLHttpRequest and invokes the PHP functions corresponding to the JavaScript wrapper functions. The default request type of PHP functions registered through Xajax is POST. The PHP functions return an XML response that is returned to the client application by the Xajax object. Based on the instructions in the XML response, the Xajax's JavaScript message pump updates the content of the client input page. Xajax has a feature that, data is updated only if data has been modified.

---

[1] Ajaxian.com- http://ajaxian.com/archives/ajaxiancom-2006-survey-results

8.2 Setting the Environment

As Xajax is a PHP class library, first download and install PHP 5. PHP 5 may be installed on different servers. We will configure PHP 5 with Apache web server on MS Windows. Download PHP[2] 5.2.4 zip file. Extract the PHP zip file to an installation directory, *C:/PHP* for example. Download Apache HTTP Server 2.0[3] *apache_2.0.x-win32-x86-no_ssl.msi* or a different version may be used. Double-click on the *.msi* file to install the Apache server. Install the Apache HTTP server.

To the PATH environment variable add *C:/PHP*, the directory in which PHP 5 is installed. Adding *C:/PHP* to the PATH variable makes *php5ts.dll* available to JDeveloper PHP extension. Rename the *php.init-recommended* file to *php.ini*.

The example application shall store and fetch data from Oracle database 10g. Therefore, enable the Oracle database extension in *php.ini* configuration file. Set the extension directory by specifying the following directive in *php.ini*.

```
extension_dir = "./ext"
```

Activate the Oracle database PHP extension by removing the ';' from the following line.

```
extension=php_oci8.dll
```

Install PHP 5 in the Apache HTTP server. To the *<Apache2>\conf\httpd.conf* file add the following directives.

```
# For PHP 5
LoadModule php5_module "C:/PHP/php5apache2.dll"
AddType application/x-httpd-php .php

# configure the path to php.ini
PHPIniDir "C:/PHP/"
```

By default, *<Apache2>* directory is the directory *C:/Program Files/Apache Group/Apache2*. If PHP is installed in a directory other than *C:/PHP*, replace *C:/PHP* with the directory in which PHP 5 is installed. Restart Apache web server after modifying the httpd.conf file.

Download Xajax0.2.4[4]. We also need to download JDeveloper 10.1.3. JDeveloper 11g is not used, because a PHP extension for JDeveloper 11g is not available.

---

[2] Download PHP- http://www.php.net/downloads.php
[3] Download Apache HTTP Server 2.0- http://httpd.apache.org/
[4] Download Xajax- http://www.xajaxproject.org/download.php

8.3 Integrating PHP with JDeveloper

After installing PHP 5 and Apache 2.0 HTTP server install the JDeveloper PHP Extension[5]. Download the PHP extension 10.1.3   zip file *oracle_jdeveloper_php.zip*. Extract the oracle.jdeveloper.php.10.1.3.jar file from the extension zip file to the *C:/JDeveloper/jdev/extensions* directory. Restart JDeveloper 10.1.3. The JDeveloper PHP extension gets installed and the new PHP File feature becomes available in **File>New>Web Tier>PHP** in **New Gallery**.

Next, specify the PHP .exe application to run PHP scripts in JDeveloper. First, create an application and project with **File>New**. In the **New Gallery** window select **General** in **Categories** and **Application** in **Items** and click on **OK**. In the **Create Application** window specify an **Application Name** and click on **OK**. In the **Create Project** window specify a **Project Name** and click on **OK**. Select the project node in **Applications-Navigator** and select **Tools>Project Properties**. In the **Project Properties** window select **PHP Runtime Settings**. In the **PHP Command-line Executable** field specify the php.exe application and click on **OK** as shown in Fig. 8.1.

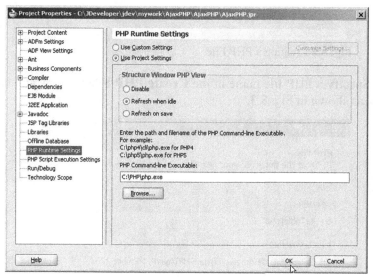

Fig. 8.1 Setting PHP Executable

---

[5]JDeveloper PHP Extension 10.1.3- http://www.oracle.com/technology/products/jdev/htdocs/partners/addins/exchange/php/index.html

Next, configure the Apache HTTP server to access the PHP scripts in a JDeveloper PHP project. Add a PHP file to the **Applications-Navigator** project with **File>New**. In the **New Gallery** window select **Web Tier>PHP** in **Categories** and **PHP File** in **Items** and click on **OK** as shown in Fig. 8.2.

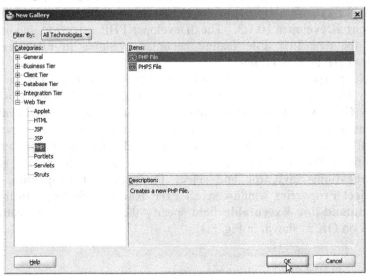

Fig. 8.2 Creating a PHP File

Specify a PHP file name in the **Create PHP File** window and click on **OK** as shown in Fig. 8.3.

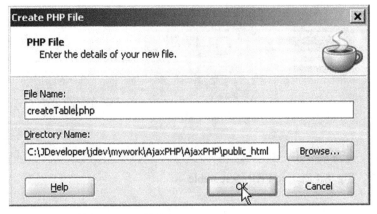

Fig. 8.3 Specifying PHP File Name

A PHP file gets added to the PHP project as shown in Fig. 8.4.

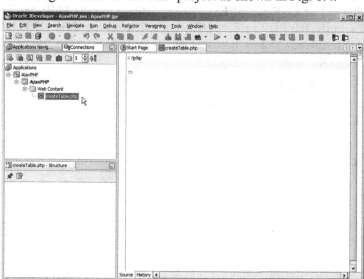

Fig. 8.4 New PHP File

Save the PHP file with **File>Save All**. Specify an `Alias` parameter in the Apache web server configuration file `httpd.conf` to map the PHP Project URL to the default PHP Project directory. In the listing shown below the first 3 lines should be on the same line in `httpd.conf` and the 2nd set of 3 lines should be on another line.

```
Alias                                        /AjaxPHP/
"C:/JDeveloper/jdev/mywork/AjaxPHP/AjaxPHP/public_ht
ml/"
<Directory
"C:/JDeveloper/jdev/mywork/AjaxPHP/AjaxPHP/public_ht
ml/">
         Options Indexes MultiViews
         AllowOverride None
         Order allow,deny
         Allow from all
</Directory>
```

Restart the Apache HTTP Server. As we have set the `public_html` directory as the PHP Project Directory, PHP scripts in the `public_html` directory shall run in the Apache server when a PHP script is invoked with the specified PHP Project URL. Next, specify the PHP Project URL to run PHP scripts in JDeveloper. Select the PHP project in the **Applications**

Navigator. Select **Tools>Project Properties**. In the **Project Properties** window select **PHP Script Execution Settings**. In the **PHP Project URL** field specify the PHP project URL and click on the **Test URL** button. If the URL directory gets accessed a "Success" message gets displayed. Click on **OK** as shown in Fig. 8.5.

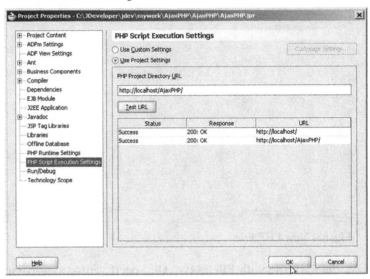

Fig. 8.5 Setting and Testing PHP Script Execution Settings

8.4 Creating a Database Table

We shall create a Xajax application to validate an input field in a form. The Xajax application retrieves data from an Oracle database table. Therefore, install Oracle database 10 g, including sample schemas. Create a database instance ORCL. Create an example database table in OE schema. The database table may be created with a PHP script.

Copy the *createTable.php* listing, which is listed below, to the *createTable.php* PHP file in JDeveloper.

```php
<?php
$username='OE';
$password='password';
$db='(DESCRIPTION =
 (ADDRESS = (PROTOCOL = TCP)(HOST = localhost)(PORT
 = 1521))
    (CONNECT_DATA =
```

```
        (SERVER = DEDICATED)
        (SERVICE_NAME = ORCL)
    )
  )';
$connection   =   oci_connect($username,   $password,
$db);
if (!$connection) {
  $e = oci_error();
  echo htmlentities($e['message']);
}
$stmt    =    oci_parse($connection,    "CREATE    TABLE
OE.Catalog(CatalogId VARCHAR(25) PRIMARY KEY, Journal
VARCHAR(25),      Publisher     Varchar(25),      Edition
VARCHAR(25),       Title      Varchar(45),       Author
Varchar(25))");
  if (!$stmt) {
    $e = oci_error($connection);
    echo htmlentities($e['message']);
  }
  $r = oci_execute($stmt);
  if (!$r) {
    $e = oci_error($stmt);
    echo htmlentities($e['message']);
  }else{
    echo $connection . " created table\n\n";
  }
$sql = "INSERT INTO OE.Catalog VALUES('catalog1',
'Oracle Magazine',    'Oracle Publishing', 'Nov-Dec
2004',    'Database   Resource   Manager',   'Kimberly
Floss')";
    $stmt = oci_parse($connection, $sql);
  if (!$stmt) {
    $e = oci_error($connection);
    echo htmlentities($e['message']);
  }
  $r = oci_execute($stmt);
  if (!$r) {
    $e = oci_error($stmt);
    echo htmlentities($e['message']);
  }else{
    echo $connection . " added a row\n\n";
  }
$sql = "INSERT INTO OE.Catalog VALUES('catalog2',
'Oracle Magazine',    'Oracle Publishing', 'Nov-Dec
2004', 'From ADF UIX to JSF', 'Jonas Jacobi')";
    $stmt = oci_parse($connection, $sql);
  if (!$stmt) {
```

```
    $e = oci_error($connection);
    echo htmlentities($e['message']);
}
$r = oci_execute($stmt);
if (!$r) {
    $e = oci_error($stmt);
    echo htmlentities($e['message']);
}else{
    echo $connection . " added a row\n\n";
}
$sql = "INSERT INTO OE.Catalog VALUES('catalog3',
'Oracle Magazine',    'Oracle Publishing', 'March-
April 2005', 'Starting with Oracle ADF ', 'Steve
Muench')";
    $stmt = oci_parse($connection, $sql);
if (!$stmt) {
    $e = oci_error($connection);
    echo htmlentities($e['message']);
}
$r = oci_execute($stmt);
if (!$r) {
    $e = oci_error($stmt);
    echo htmlentities($e['message']);
}else{
    echo $connection . " added a row\n\n";
}
?>
```

If the HOST, PORT or SERVICE_NAME are different than those
specified in the PHP script, modify the settings in the script. Start Apache
web server, if not already started. Run the PHP script in JDeveloper.
Right-click on *createTable.php* and select Run as shown in Fig. 8.6

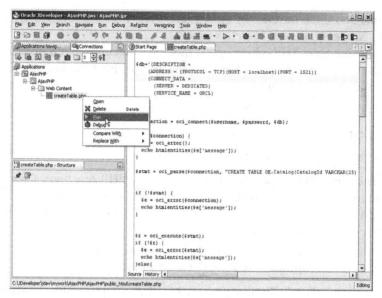

Fig. 8.6 Running a PHP Script

A database table, `Catalog`, gets generated and data gets added to the table.

8.5 Sending an Ajax Request

We shall develop an example application comprising of an input form. The input form takes data to add a catalog entry to database table `Catalog`. As a user begins to enter data in the input field Catalog Id, a `XMLHttpRequest` is sent to the server to validate the Catalog Id value added. If the Catalog Id is not already defined in the database, a message "Catalog Id is Valid" gets displayed. If the Catalog Id is already defined in the database, a message "Catalog Id is not Valid" gets displayed, the **Create Catalog** button gets disabled and field values for the Catalog Id get added to the form. We have used business logic that if a catalog id is not already defined the catalog id is valid. Additional business logic may be added to match the catalog id with a PHP regular expression.

Extract *xajax_0.2.4.zip* file to the `public_html` directory of the PHP Ajax project in JDeveloper. Rename the *xajax_0.2.4* directory to *xajax*. Create a PHP script in the PHP Ajax project. Select **File>New**. In the **New Gallery** window select **Web Tier>PHP** in **Categories**. Select **PHP File** in

Items and click on **OK**. In the **Create PHP File** window specify a PHP **File Name**, *input.php*, and click on **OK**.

The `xajax` PHP object performs the function of an intermediary between the client application and the server. First, include the `xajax` class library in *input.php*.

```
require('./xajax/xajax.inc.php');
```

Create a `xajax` object.

```
$xajax = new xajax();
```

The server side processing is performed by PHP functions. Create PHP functions `validateCatalogId($formValues)` and `updateCatalog($formValues)`. Both these functions take a `$formValues` parameter.

```
function validateCatalogId($formValues){}
function updateCatalog($formValues){}
```

Register the PHP functions with the `xajax` object using the `registerFunction()` method. The `xajax` object creates wrapper functions for the PHP functions that may be invoked from a PHP script or an input form event handler.

```
$xajax->registerFunction("validateCatalogId");
$xajax->registerFunction("updateCatalog");
```

Xajax generates asynchronous wrapper functions for the registered PHP functions. A wrapper function name is of the format: `xajax_<phpfunction>`. Variable `<phpfunction>` is a server side PHP function for which a wrapper function is to be defined. Xajax provides asynchronous form processing with the `getFormValues(string formId)` method. Using the `getFormValues()` method, an array of form field values may be submitted as an argument to a xajax asynchronous function. Sections of a form may also be submitted instead of the complete form with the `getFormValues(string formID ,boolean submitDisabledElements, string prefix])` function. The `prefix` parameter specifies that only form elements starting with that prefix should be submitted. Boolean parameter `submitDisabledElements` specifies if disabled elements are to be submitted. . PHP functions `validateCatalogId` and `updateCatalog` define a parameter for an array of form field values. Before an `XMLHttpRequest` is initiated, specify the `xajax` object to handle requests with the `processRequests()` function.

```
$xajax->processRequests();
```

Also specify in the `<head></head>` tags of the input form that Xajax should generate any required JavaScript after an XML response has been sent back from the server.

```
<?php $xajax->printJavascript('./xajax');
?>
```

An `XMLHttpRequest` is initiated by a client application. In the example application, an `XMLHttpRequest` is initiated by the `onkeyup` event handler in input field `catalogId`.

```
<tr><td>Catalog Id:</td><td><input      type="text"
            size="20"
             id="catalogId"
             name="catalogId"
      autocomplete="off"
onkeyup="xajax_validateCatalogId(xajax.getFormValue
s('validationForm'));"></td>
<td><div id="validationMessage"></div></td>
</tr>
```

The Catalog Id input field invokes the wrapper function `xajax_validateCatalogId` with an array of form field values as a parameter. The wrapper functions send an `XMLHttpRequest` to the server. The `xajax` object receives the `XMLHttpRequest` and invokes the corresponding PHP function `validateCatalogId($formValues)`.

8.6 Processing an Ajax Request

Xajax provides the `xajaxResponse` class to send a response to the client application. In the `validateCatalogId` function, create a `xajaxResponse` object.

```
$objResponse = new xajaxResponse();
```

The `validateCatalogId` function validates a Catalog Id value added in the input form. From the `$formValues` array retrieve the value of the `catalogId` field.

```
$catalogId=trim($formValues['catalogId']);
```

Next, we shall use the PHP Oracle extension to connect with the Oracle database and determine if a `Catalog` table row is defined for the catalog id value input in the input form. Define variables `$username`,

$password, and $db for Oracle database username, password and database. Specify the $db variable value as the database SID value in the <Oracle10g>/NETWORK/ADMIN/tnsnames.ora file.

```
$username='OE';
$password='';

$db='(DESCRIPTION =
    (ADDRESS = (PROTOCOL = TCP)(HOST =localhost)(PORT
= 1521))
    (CONNECT_DATA =
      (SERVER = DEDICATED)
      (SERVICE_NAME = ORCL)
    )
  )';
```

Obtain a connection with the database using oci_connect function.

```
$connection = oci_connect($username, $password, $db);
```

Prepare an Oracle statement to select a row of data for the catalog id value input in the form. The oci_parse(conection, query) function is used to compile a statement.

```
$stmt = oci_parse($connection, "SELECT * from
OE.CATALOG WHERE catalogId='".$catalogId."'");
```

Run the SQL query with the oci_execute(statement) function.

```
$r = oci_execute($stmt);
```

Fetch the rows in the result set using the oci_fetch_all(statement, result) function.

```
$nrows = oci_fetch_all($stmt, $result);
```

The oci_fetch_all function returns the number of rows in the result set. If the result set is empty, a Catalog table row for the catalog id value is not defined in the database table. Therefore, the Catalog Id field value added in the form is valid. Next, we shall generate a response to be sent to the client application. A response contains one or more command messages. Some of the commonly used command messages are discussed in Table 8.1.

Table 8.1 xajaxResponse Command Messages

Command Message	Description
Assign	Sets the specified attribute of an element in input page with the method addAssign(string elementId, string attribute, string data)
Append	Appends data to the specified attribute of an element in the input page with the method addAppend(string elementId, string attribute, string data)
Prepend	Prepends data to the specified attribute of an element in the input page with the method addPrepend(string elementId, string attribute, string data)
Replace	Replaces data in the specified attribute of an element in the input page with the method addReplace(string elementId, string attribute, string replace, string data)
Script	Runs the specified JavaScript code with method addScript(string javascript)
Alert	Displays an alert box with the specified message with the method addAlert(string message)

If the number of rows in the result set obtained with the Catalog Id value specified in the input form is zero, display a message in the validationMessage div, "Catalog Id is Valid". The addAssign method sets the innerHTML of the validationMessage div.

```
$objResponse-
>addAssign("validationMessage","innerHTML","Catalog
Id is Valid");
```

If the result has rows, the catalog id value is defined in the Catalog table. Therefore, the Catalog Id value added in the input form is not valid. If number of rows in the result set is more than zero, set the innerHTML of the validationMessage div to "Catalog Id is not Valid".

```
$objResponse-
>addAssign("validationMessage","innerHTML","Catalog
Id is not Valid");
```

Next, fetch values from the result set and set the values in the input form fields. Retrieve field values from the result set using column name and Array index (0 based). For example, the journal column value is obtained with PHP code shown below.

```
$journal=$result['JOURNAL'][0];
```

Set the value attribute of the input form field elements with addAssign method. For example, the value attribute of the journal element is set as shown below.

```
$objResponse->addAssign("journal","value",$journal);
```

Also disable the submit button.

```
$objResponse-
>addAssign("submitForm","disabled",true);
```

Return the $objResponse object from the validateCatalogId function as an XML string.

```
return $objResponse->getXML();
```

8.7 Processing the Ajax Response

The XML response is sent to the xajax processor, which sends the XML response to the xajax's JavaScript message pump. The message pump parses the XML instructions and sets the elements in the input page. Thus, the data specified in the $xmlResponse object with addAssign method is set in the input form.

The updateCatalog($formValues) function is used to update database table Catalog from the input form. If the Catalog Id field value is valid, a new catalog entry may be created by adding values to the other fields of the form. Click on the **Create Catalog** button to submit the form. The onsubmit event handler invokes the wrapper function xajax_updateCatalog, which sends an XMLHttpRequest to the server.

```
onsubmit="xajax_updateCatalog(xajax.getFormValues('v
alidationForm'));"
```

The xajax object receives the XMLHttpRequest and invokes the corresponding PHP function updateCatalog($formValues). In the updateCatalog function, retrieve the form field values and create an SQL statement to add a row to database table Catalog. Obtain a connection with the database and run the SQL statement. The *input.php* script is listed below.

```
<?php require('./xajax/xajax.inc.php');
$xajax = new xajax();
$xajax->cleanBufferOn();
$xajax->registerFunction("validateCatalogId");
$xajax->registerFunction("updateCatalog");
function validateCatalogId($formValues){
$objResponse = new xajaxResponse();
$catalogId=trim($formValues['catalogId']);
$username='OE';
```

```php
$password='password';
$db=' (DESCRIPTION =
    (ADDRESS   =   (PROTOCOL   =   TCP)(HOST   =
localhost)(PORT = 1521))
    (CONNECT_DATA =
       (SERVER = DEDICATED)
       (SERVICE_NAME = ORCL)
    )
  )';
$connection = oci_connect($username, $password, $db);
$stmt   =   oci_parse($connection,   "SELECT   *   from
OE.CATALOG WHERE catalogId='".$catalogId."'");
$r = oci_execute($stmt);
$nrows = oci_fetch_all($stmt, $result);
if($nrows==0){
$objResponse-
>addAssign("validationMessage","innerHTML","Catalog
Id is Valid");
$objResponse-
>addAssign("submitForm","disabled",false);
$objResponse->addAssign("journal","value","");
$objResponse->addAssign("publisher","value","");
$objResponse->addAssign("edition","value","");
$objResponse->addAssign("title","value","");
$objResponse->addAssign("author","value","");
}
if($nrows>0){
$objResponse-
>addAssign("validationMessage","innerHTML","Catalog
Id is not Valid");
$catalogId=$result['CATALOGID'][0];
$journal=$result['JOURNAL'][0];
$publisher=$result['PUBLISHER'][0];
$edition=$result['EDITION'][0];
$title=$result['TITLE'][0];
$author=$result['AUTHOR'][0];
$objResponse->addAssign("journal","value",$journal);
$objResponse-
>addAssign("publisher","value",$publisher);
$objResponse->addAssign("edition","value",$edition);
$objResponse->addAssign("title","value",$title);
$objResponse->addAssign("author","value",$author);
$objResponse-
>addAssign("submitForm","disabled",true);
}
return $objResponse->getXML();
}
```

```php
function updateCatalog($formValues){
$catalogId=trim($formValues['catalogId']);
$journal=trim($formValues['journal']);
$publisher=trim($formValues['publisher']);
$edition=trim($formValues['edition']);
$title=trim($formValues['title']);
$author=trim($formValues['author']);
$username='OE';
$password='password';
$db='(DESCRIPTION =
    (ADDRESS    =    (PROTOCOL    =    TCP)(HOST    =
localhost)(PORT = 1521))
    (CONNECT_DATA =
       (SERVER = DEDICATED)
       (SERVICE_NAME = ORCL)
    )
  )';
$connection = oci_connect($username, $password, $db);
$sql = "INSERT INTO OE.Catalog
VALUES('".$catalogId."','".$journal."','".$publisher.
"','".$edition."','".$title."','".$author."')";
$stmt = oci_parse($connection, $sql);
$r=oci_execute($stmt);
if (!$r) {
  $e = oci_error($stmt);
  echo htmlentities($e['message']);
}
}
$xajax->processRequests();
?>
<head>
<?php $xajax->printJavascript('./xajax');
?>
</head>
<body>
<h1>Form to Create a Catalog Entry</h1>
<form    id="validationForm"        name="validationForm"
onsubmit="xajax_updateCatalog(xajax.getFormValues('va
lidationForm'));">
<table>
<tr><td>Catalog Id:</td><td><input     type="text"
              size="20"
                id="catalogId"
              name="catalogId"
onkeyup="xajax_validateCatalogId(xajax.getFormValues(
'validationForm'));"></td>
<td><div id="validationMessage"></div></td>
```

```
</tr>
<tr><td>Journal:</td><td><input     type="text"
          size="20"
           id="journal"
          name="journal"></td>
</tr>
<tr><td>Publisher:</td><td><input     type="text"
          size="20"
           id="publisher"
          name="publisher"></td>
</tr>
<tr><td>Edition:</td><td><input     type="text"
          size="20"
           id="edition"
          name="edition"></td>
</tr>
<tr><td>Title:</td><td><input     type="text"
          size="20"
           id="title"
          name="title"></td>
</tr>
<tr><td>Author:</td><td><input     type="text"
          size="20"
           id="author"
          name="author"></td>
</tr>
<tr><td><input     type="submit"
          value="Create Catalog"
           id="submitForm"
          name="submitForm"></td>
</tr>
</table>
</form>
</body>
</html>
```

Copy the *input.php* listing to the *input.php* file in PHP Ajax project in JDeveloper. Next, run the *input.php* script in the Apache web server. Right-click on *input.php* and select **Run** as shown in Fig. 8.7.

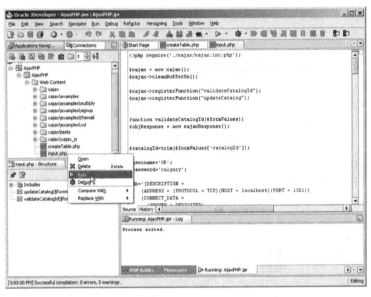

Fig. 8.7 Running Xajax Application

The input form gets displayed. Start adding a value for the Catalog Id field. An XMLHttpRequest request is sent to the server with each addition to the text field. The input page gets updated with response from the server that contains instructions about the validity of the Catalog Id. A message gets displayed to verify if the Catalog Id field value is valid as shown in Fig. 8.8.

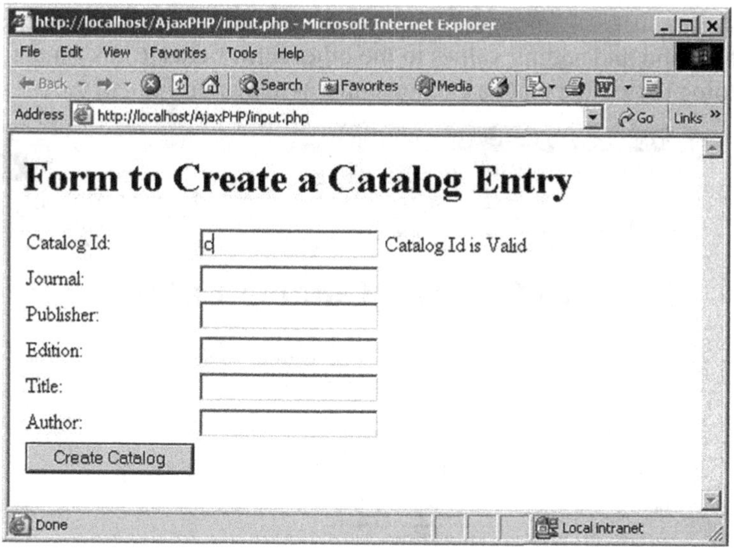

Fig. 8.8 Validating Catalog Id

If a value is specified that is already defined in the Catalog table, a message "Catalog Id is not Valid" gets displayed. For example, add `catalog1` to Catalog Id field. As `catalog1` is already defined the "not valid" message gets displayed as shown in Fig. 8.9.

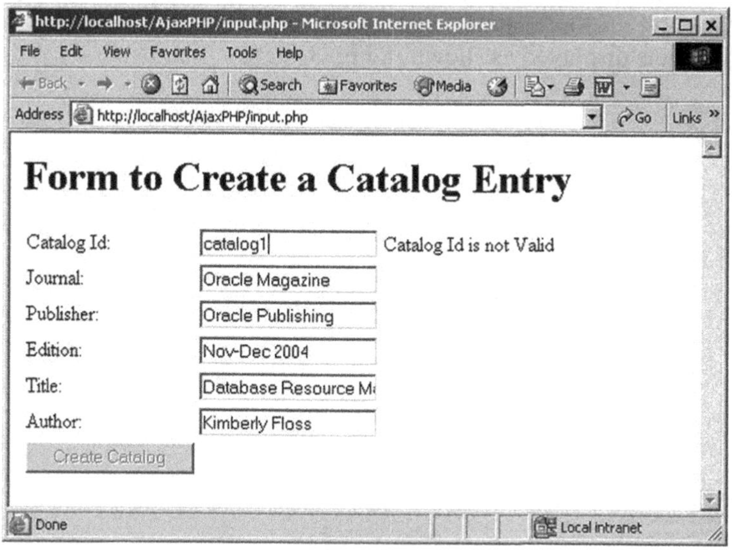

Fig. 8.9 Non Valid Catalog Id

A new catalog entry may be created by specifying a Catalog Id field that is valid and adding values to the other form fields. Click on the **Create Catalog** button to create a catalog entry as shown in Fig. 8.10.

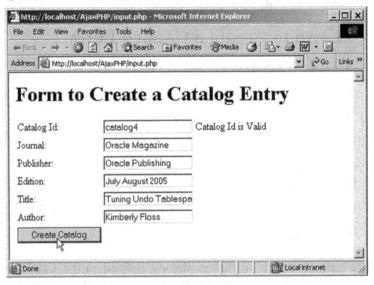

Fig. 8.10 Creating a Catalog Entry

If Catalog Id field previously used to create a catalog entry, catalog4 in the example, is specified a message, "Catalog Id is not Valid", gets displayed as shown in Fig. 8.11.

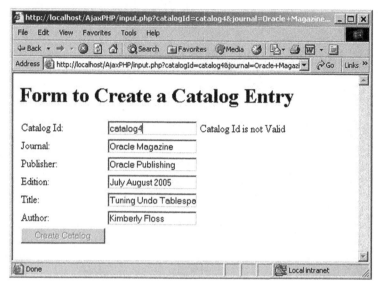

Fig. 8.11 Catalog Id becomes Non Valid after a Catalog entry is created

8.8 Summary

PHP may be used with Ajax either by directly specifying a PHP script URL in the open() method of the XMLHttpRequest object or with a PHP framework for Ajax. JDeveloper 10g provides an extension for PHP for running PHP files in JDeveloper. Xajax is a PHP Ajax framework. In this chapter we is configured the PHP extension for JDeveloper in JDeveloper 10g. Using Xajax we sent an Ajax request from an input form to create a catalog entry. Ajax is used to validate a catalog id for creating a new catalog entry. Using the Ajax response a validation message is displayed to indicate the validity of a catalog id.

9 RSS Feed with Ajax

9.1 Introduction

RSS is a collection of web feed formats, specified in XML, used to provide frequently updated digital content to users. RSS is an acronym with different representations for different standards; for RSS 2.0, Really Simple Syndication, for RSS 0.91 and RSS 1.0, Rich Site Summary, for RSS 0.9 and RSS 1.0, RDF Site Summary. RSS Google provides the Google AJAX Feed API to receive any RSS feed. The Google Ajax Feed API supports the following RSS feed formats: RSS 2.0, RSS 1.0, RSS 0.94, RSS 0.93, RSS 0.92, RSS 0.91, and RSS 0.9. An RSS Feed may be displayed in JSON Result Format, XML Result Format, or combined JSON/XML Result Format. JSON (JavaScript Object Notation) is a data interchange format used to transmit structured data. JSON is based on the following data structures.

1. Object-Collection of key-value pairs, separated by a comma, and enclosed in {}.
2. Array-Ordered sequence of values, separated by a comma and enclosed in [].

For example, the following JSON represents a catalog object.

```
{
    "journal": "Oracle Magazine",
    "publisher": "Oracle Publishing",
    "edition": "January-February 2007",
    "title": "Know Your UML with XML",
    "author": [
        "Robert Wigetman",
        "Jurgen Moortgat"
    ]
}
```

By default the Ajax Feed API returns the feed in JSON format. Because of the incompatibilities between the various versions of RSS and the limitations of RSS, a new syndication specification, Atom, was introduced in 2003. Atom feed has advantages over the RSS feed. RSS is an approximate subset of Atom. Both Atom and RSS have features not provided by the other. RSS feed supports only plain text and HTML, whereas Atom feed supports various additional content types such as XHTML, XML and binary, and references to video and audio content. Atom is a standardized by IETF, whereas RSS is not standardized. Atom supports XML standard features such as XML Schema, RSS doesn't. Atom is in an XML namespace while RSS 2.0 is not. Microsoft has introduced the Simple Sharing Extensions (SSE), which extend the Atom 1.0 and RSS 2.0 specifications to provide item sharing between cross-subscribed feeds.

9.2 Overview of Google Ajax Feed API

A Google Ajax Feed is represented by the `google.feeds.Feed` class. The `Feed` class has the methods discussed in Table 9.1. The `Feed` class methods do not have a return type.

Table 9.1 Feed Class Methods

Method	Description
load(callbackFunction)	Downloads the feed from the Google server. The callbackFunction gets invoked when the download is complete. The callbackFunction is invoked with a argument that represents the result of the feed.
setNumEntries(num)	Sets the number of feed entries. Default value is 4.
setResultFormat(format)	Sets the result format. One of the following values may be specified: google.feeds.Feed.JSON_FORMAT (the default), google.feeds.Feed.XML_FORMAT, or google.feeds.Feed.MIXED_FORMAT.

The Google Ajax Feed API generates a result document, whose structure is different from either the RSS 2.0 or the Atom 1.0 feed. For example, the chapter mentions elements such `contentSnippet` and `publishedDate`. Neither Atom 1.0 nor RSS 2.0 have these elements. The `contentSnippet` element corresponds to the snippet version of the `content` or `summary` element in Atom 1.0 and `description` element in RSS 2.0. The `publishedDate` element corresponds to the published element in Atom and the pubDate element in RSS 2.0. Google Feed API uses its own set of result elements to generate a uniform result format for the Atom 1.0 feed and the RSS 2.0 feed, which have some of the elements different. The Google Ajax feed applications in this chapter may be used with either the RSS 2.0 feed or the Atom 1.0 feed. The URL for the RSS 2.0 feed would be different from the Atom 1.0 feed though.

The root element of the result is root. If the loading generates an error, the root element has an error sub-element. The error element has sub-elements code and message. The code element specifies the error code and the message element specifies the description of the error. If the result format is JSON_FORMAT or MIXED_FORMAT the root element has a sub-element called feed. If the result format is XML_FORMAT or MIXED_FORMAT the root element has an element called xmlDocument. The xmlDocument element contains the XML document for the feed. For JSON result format the feed element has the sub-elements discussed in Table 9.2.

Table 9.2 Sub-Elements of feed

Sub-Element	Description
title	Specifies the feed title.
link	Specifies the URL of the HTML version of the feed.
description	Specifies the feed description.
author	Specifies the feed author.
entries[]	One or more entries may be present. Each entry has the following sub-elements: title-The entry title. link-URL of the HTML version of the entry. content- Specifies content of the entry including HTML tags. contentSnippet-A snippet version of the content. publishedDate-Date of publication. categories[]-One or more category String tags.

For google.feeds.Feed.MIXED_FORMAT result format both the feed and xmlDocument sub-elements are present in the root element. An additional sub-element called xmlNode is present for each entry for MIXED_FORMAT. The xmlNode sub-element is a pointer to the XML element in the XML document in the xmlElement element.

The google.feeds.FeedControl class is used to download and display multiple feeds. The FeedControl methods are discussed in Table 9.3.

Table 9.3 FeedControl Methods

Method	Description
addFeed(url, label)	Adds the feed specified by the url to the FeedControl.
draw(element, opt_options?)	Loads the feeds and displays the feeds. The element argument specifies the DOM node that contains the resulting entries. The optional opt_options specifies the control options as a JSON object to display the results. The object has a single property called drawMode, which has the value google.feeds.FeedControl.DRAW_MODE_TABBED or google.feeds.FeedControl.DRAW_MODE_LINEAR (default).
setNumEntries(num)	Specifies the number of entries for each feed. Default value is 4.
setLinkTarget(linkTarget)	Specifies the link target to display the HTML for an entry. The following values may be specified: google.feeds.LINK_TARGET_BLANK google.feeds.LINK_TARGET_SELF (default) google.feeds.LINK_TARGET_TOP google.feeds.LINK_TARGET_PARENT

Google Ajax Feed API provides a global method `google.feeds.getElementsByTagNameNS(node, ns, localName)`, which returns a `NodeList` of elements of the specified local name and namespace URI.

9.3 Setting the Environment

We need to develop a JavaScript application to download and display RSS feeds with the Google AJAX Feed API. We need to register a web application URL with the Google AJAX Feed API to download and display RSS feed. We shall create a JavaScript application in JDeveloper. Download and install JDeveloper 11g. To create a JDeveloper application select **File>New** and subsequently select **General** in **Categories** and **Application** in **Items** in the **New Gallery** window. Click on **OK**. In the **Create Application** window specify an **Application Name** and click on **OK**. In the **Create Project** window specify a **Project Name** and click on **OK**. A new application and project get added to the **Applications-Navigator**. Add a HTML page to the JDeveloper project by selecting the project node and selecting **File>New**. In the **New Gallery** window   select

Web Tier>HTML in **Categories** and **HTML Page** in **Items**. Click on **OK**. In the **Create HTML File** window specify a **File Name** and click on **OK**. An HTML page gets added as shown in Fig. 9.1.

Fig. 9.1 RSS Ajax Application

We need to register the URL for the HTML page with the Google AJAX Feed API. Right-click on the HTML page and select **Run**. Obtain the URL, which is `http://127.0.0.1:8988/RSSAjax-RSSAjax-context-root/`. Sign up for the Google AJAX Feed API using the URL *http://code.google.com/apis/ajaxfeeds/signup.html.* as shown in Fig. 9.2. Click on the **Generate API Key** button to generate the API key. You would need to be logged in to your Google user account to generate an API key. The generated Google AJAX Feed API key may be used with all the URLs in the directory `http://127.0.0.1:8988/RSSAjax-RSSAjax-context-root/`.

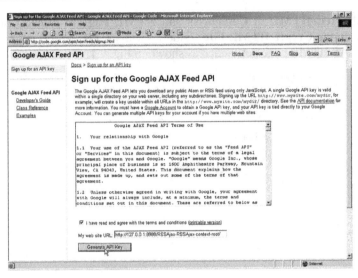

Fig. 9.2 Generating Google Feed API key

9.4 Receiving a RSS Feed

In this section we shall generate a JavaScript application to download and display JDeveloper RSS feed.. First, obtain the URL for the JDeveloper RSS   feed   from *http://www.oracle.com/technology/products/jdev/temp/whatisrss.html.*
The   URL   for   the   JDeveloper   RSS   feed   is `http://www.oracle.com/technology/products/jdev/jde veloper_news.xml`. First, to access a Feed with the Google AJAX Feed API we need to add the following `script` element, which specifies the Google AJAX Feed API key, to the JavaScript application *RSSAjax.html.*

```
<script type="text/javascript"
src="http://www.google.com/jsapi?key=ABQIAAAAItA
EL-H-GuOHsDfD7MxmlhTrOhjqk34-
mQfF8ylMFkKrUrP8PBQp_aNLt1q7hnvFFrJPCESK3bbSVQ">
</script>
```

The `script` tag loads the `google.load` function that is required to load individual Google APIs. Download version 1 of the `feeds` API.

```
google.load("feeds", "1");
```

Create a JavaScript function initialize and specify the function to be invoked when the Google Feed API has loaded.

```
google.setOnLoadCallback(initialize);
```

Create a Feed class object to download a feed. Specify the URL for the JDeveloper RSS Feed to create the Feed class object.

```
var feed = new google.feeds.Feed
("http://www.oracle.com/technology/products/
jdev/jdeveloper_news.xml");
```

Load the RSS feed using the load(callbackFunction) method of the Feed class.

```
feed.load(function(result) {          });
```

Add a div element to the body element of the JavaScript application to display the RSS feed results.

```
<body><div id="feed"></div></body>
```

In the callback function obtain the div element using the getElementById method.

```
var container = document.getElementById("feed");
```

Iterate over the feed results.

```
for (var i = 0; i < result.feed.entries.length;
i++) {          }
```

Obtain each of the feed entries, create a div element for each of the feed entries and add the entry title to the div element for each of the feed entries.

```
var entry = result.feed.entries[i];
var div=document.createElement("div");
div.appendChild(document.createTextNode(entry.title))
;
```

Add the div element for each of the entries to the container div element.

```
container.appendChild(div);
```

Copy the RSS Ajax JavaScript application. *RSSAjax.html*, shown below, to *RSSAjax.html* in JDeveloper.

```
<!DOCTYPE    html    PUBLIC    "-//W3C//DTD    XHTML    1.0
Strict//EN"    "http://www.w3.org/TR/xhtml1/DTD/xhtml1-
strict.dtd">
<html xmlns="http://www.w3.org/1999/xhtml">
<head>
<meta   http-equiv="content-type"   content="text/html;
charset=utf-8"/>
<title>Google AJAX Feed API - Simple Example</title>
    <script type="text/javascript"
src="http://www.google.com/jsapi?key=ABQIAAAAItAEL-H-
GuOHsDfD7MxmlhTrOhjqk34-
mQfF8ylMFkKrUrP8PBQp_aNLt1q7hnvFFrJPCESK3bbSVQ"></scr
ipt>
<script                            type="text/javascript">
google.load("feeds", "1");       function initialize()
{var           feed           =           new
google.feeds.Feed("http://www.oracle.com/technology/p
roducts/jdev/jdeveloper_news.xml");
feed.load(function(result) {        if (!result.error)
{var   container   =   document.getElementById("feed");
for (var i = 0; i < result.feed.entries.length; i++)
{              var entry = result.feed.entries[i];
var       div       =       document.createElement("div");
div.appendChild(document.createTextNode(entry.title))
; container.appendChild(div);              }              }
});        }         google.setOnLoadCallback(initialize);
</script>
    </head>
    <body><div id="feed"></div></body>
</html>
```

To display the RSS Feed entries' titles, right-click on the *RSSAjax.html*
HTML page and select **Run** as shown in Fig. 9.3.

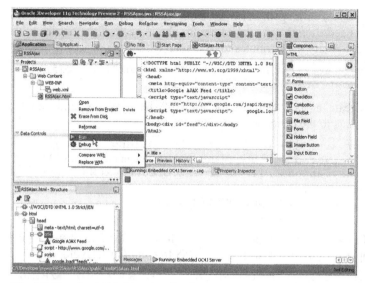

Fig. 9.3 Running RSS Ajax Application

The entries' titles in the RSS feed get displayed as shown in Fig. 9.4.

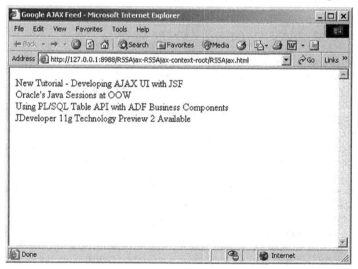

Fig. 9.4 RSS Feed Titles

The preceding RSS Feed application only displays the titles of the entries in the RSS feed. Next, we shall display additional JSON properties such as `link`, `publishedDate` and `contentSnippet` from the RSS Feed. Iterate over the entries to obtain each of the entries in the RSS Feed Specify the attributes to be displayed.

```
var attributes = ["title", "link", "publishedDate",
"contentSnippet"];
```

Create a `div` element for each of the attributes and add the `div` elements to the container `div` element.

```
for (var j = 0; j < attributes.length; j++) {
    var div = document.createElement("div");
  div.appendChild(document.createTextNode(entry[attri
butes[j]]));
    container.appendChild(div);
}
```

Copy the JavaScript application, listed below, to display the JSON properties from the RSS Feed, to *RSSAjax.html* in JDeveloper.

```
<!DOCTYPE  html  PUBLIC  "-//W3C//DTD  XHTML  1.0
Strict//EN"  "http://www.w3.org/TR/xhtml1/DTD/xhtml1-
strict.dtd">
<html xmlns="http://www.w3.org/1999/xhtml">
  <head>
   <meta                    http-equiv="content-type"
   content="text/html; charset=utf-8"/>
    <title>Google   AJAX   Feed   API   -   Simple
    Example</title>
    <script type="text/javascript"
  src="http://www.google.com/jsapi?key=ABQIAAAAItAEL-
H-GuOHsDfD7MxmlhTrOhjqk34-
mQfF8ylMFkKrUrP8PBQp_aNLt1q7hnvFFrJPCESK3bbSVQ"></scr
ipt>
<script                    type="text/javascript">
google.load("feeds", "1");     function initialize()
{var            feed            =            new
google.feeds.Feed("http://feeds.feedburner.com/time/n
ation");
  feed.load(function(result) {
    if (!result.error) {
  var container = document.getElementById("feed");
    for (var i = 0; i < result.feed.entries.length;
    i++) {
        var entry = result.feed.entries[i];
        var     attributes     =     ["title",    "link",
   "publishedDate", "contentSnippet"];
        for (var j = 0; j < attributes.length; j++) {
```

```
var div = document.createElement("div");
div.appendChild(document.createTextNode(entry[attri
butes[j]]));
        container.appendChild(div);
      }
    }}
}); }
google.setOnLoadCallback(initialize);
</script>
 </head>
 <body><div id="feed"></div></body>
</html>
```

Run the *RSSAjax.html* application. The RSS Feed entry's title, link and publication date get displayed as shown in Fig. 9.5.

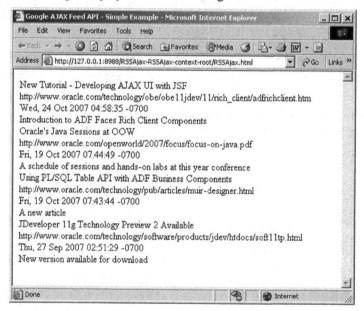

Fig. 9.5 JSON RSS Feed

9.5 Receiving Multiple Feeds

The Google Ajax Feed API may be used to display multiple feeds. Next, we shall display multiple feeds using the `FeedControl` class. We shall display the JDeveloper RSS feed and the Application Express News RSS feed. As in the JavaScript application to display a single feed specify a `script` tag for the Google Feed APIs. Add a `div` element to the JavaScript application to display the RSS Feeds.

```
<body><div id="feedControl">Loading</div></body>
```

Load version 1 of the Feed API. Invoke a callback function initialize after the Google Feed API has loaded. In the callback function create a `FeedControl` object.

```
var feedControl = new google.feeds.FeedControl();
```

Specify the RSS Feeds to be loaded by the `FeedControl`.

```
feedControl.addFeed("http://www.oracle.com/technology
/products/jdev/jdeveloper_news.xml", "JDeveloper");
   feedControl.addFeed("http://www.oracle.com/technolo
gy/products/database/application_express/news/apex.rs
s.xml", "Application Express");
```

Load the RSS Feeds and display the RSS Feeds using the `draw` method.

```
feedControl.draw(document.getElementById("feedControl
"));
```

Copy the JavaScript application, *RSSAjax.html* listed below, to load multiple RSS Feeds to *RSSAjax.html* in JDeveloper.

```
<html>
    <head>
       <script type="text/javascript"
src="http://www.google.com/jsapi?key=ABQIAAAAItAEL-H-
GuOHsDfD7MxmlhTrOhjqk34-
mQfF8ylMFkKrUrP8PBQp_aNLt1q7hnvFFrJPCESK3bbSVQ"></scr
ipt><script type="text/javascript">
        google.load("feeds", "1");
        function initialize() {
var feedControl = new google.feeds.FeedControl();
feedControl.addFeed("http://www.oracle.com/technology
/products/jdev/jdeveloper_news.xml", "JDeveloper");
   feedControl.addFeed("http://www.oracle.com/technolo
gy/products/database/application_express/news/apex.rs
s.xml ", "Application Express");
feedControl.draw(document.getElementById("feedControl
"));
}google.setOnLoadCallback(initialize);
</script></head>
    <body><div id="feedControl">Loading</div></body>
    </html>
```

Run the JavaScript application. Right-click on *RSSAjax.html* and select **Run** as shown in Fig. 9.6.

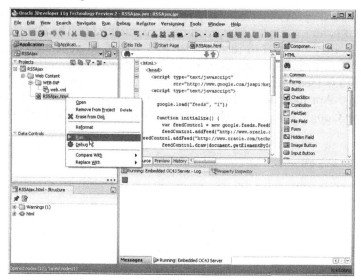

Fig. 9.6 Running Multiple Feed Application

Multiple RSS feeds get displayed as shown in Fig. 9.7.

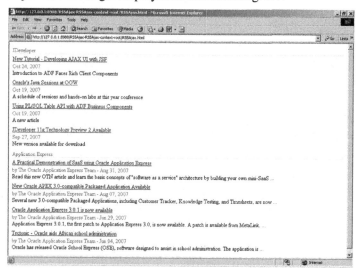

Fig. 9.7 Multiple RSS Feeds

9.6 Summary

RSS 2.0 feed provides frequently updated digital content as web feed. Atom 1.0 is an incremental improvement over RSS 2.0. The Google Ajax Feed API may be used to read a web feed. The feed generated with the Google Ajax Feed API has a set of elements that is different from either the RSS 2.0 feed elements or the Atom 1.0 feed elements. The Google Ajax Feed Api may be used to retrieve either the RSS feed or the Atom feed. The Google Ajax Feed API may also be used to read multiple feeds.

10 Web Search with Ajax

10.1 Introduction

Ajax is the web technique to refresh content on a web page without reposting the web page. We have used Ajax to submit an input form to retrieve/create a catalog entry. Ajax may also be added to web search. Google Ajax Search API and Yahoo Search Web Services add Ajax to web search. Google Ajax Search API provides a search control and various searchers to specialize the web search. For example, using the Google Local Search service the web search may be localized to a specified region. The Google Blog search service is used to search only blogs. Yahoo Search Web Services provides Web Services that may be included in web applications to generate dynamic content for an input. In this chapter we shall add Ajax to web search using the Google Ajax search API and the Yahoo Search Web Services in JDeveloper 11g.

10.2 Setting the Environment for Google Search

Before we may start using the Google Ajax Search API we need to create a web application and register the URL of the web application with the Google Ajax Search. Create a JDeveloper application and project with **File>New**. In the **New Gallery** window select **General** in **Categories** and **Application** in **Items** and click on **OK**. Add a JSP, ajaxsearch.jsp, to the JDeveloper project with **File>New**. In the **New Gallery** window select **Web Tier>JSP** in **Categories** and **JSP** in **Items** and click on **OK**. In the **Create JSP** window specify a file name and click on **OK**. The directory structure of the Google Search application is shown in Fig. 10.1.

Fig. 10.1 Web Application for Google Ajax Search

To obtain the URL for the *ajaxsearch.jsp* JSP right-click on the JSP and select **Run**. The URL for the *ajaxsearch.jsp* JSP is `http://127.0.0.1:8988/GoogleAjax-GoogleAjax-context-root/`. Next, we shall register the URL with Google Ajax Search. In the **Sign-up for an   AJAX Search API key page** (*http://code.google.com/apis/ajaxsearch/signup.html*) specify the web application URL in the **My web site URL** field, and click on **Generate API Key** button as shown in Fig. 10.2.

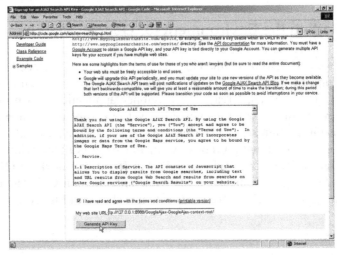

Fig. 10.2 Registering with Google AJAX Search API

Sign in to the Google account if not already signed in. A Google Ajax Search API key gets generated that may be used only for the web application for which the URL is registered. Save a copy of the Google Ajax Search API key for use in a Google Ajax search application.

10.3 Overview of Google Ajax Search API

The main class of the Google Ajax search API is GSearchControl, which provides the user interface for a search performs the search using the different searcher objects. Some of the commonly used methods of the GSearchControl class are discussed in Table 10.1.

Table 10.1 GSearchControl Methods

Method	Description
addSearcher	Adds a searcher to the search control object.
draw	Binds the search control object to the HTML container. The search results are displayed in a specified DOM element.
execute	Initiates a search across the different searchers specified in the search control using a specified search term.
setResultSetSize	Sets the result set size. Specifies the number of results in the result set. Values that may be specified are GSearch.LARGE_RESULTSET, which corresponds to 8 results, and GSearch.SMALL_RESULTSET, which corresponds to 4 results.
clearAllResults	Clears all the search results from the search control.
setLinkTarget	Specifies the link target for links embedded in search results. Default value is GSearch.LINK_TARGET_BLANK, which opens a link in a new window.
setSearchCompleteCallback	Specifies a callback method that is invoked when the search is complete.
setSearchStartingCallback	Specifies a callback method that is invoked when the search begins.

The search services are provided by searchers, which are represented by the GSearch class. The different searchers that are provided are discussed in Table 10.2.

Table 10.2 Searchers

Searcher	Description
GwebSearch	Provides the Google web search service. The search may be restricted to a specific web site, such as Expedia.com, using the setSiteRestriction method.
GlocalSearch	Provides the local search service. The location for the search may be specified using GPoint, GMap or a string.
GvideoSearch	Provides the Google Video Search service.
GblogSearch	Provides the Google Blog Search Service.
GnewsSearch	Provides the Google New Service.
GbookSearch	Provides the Google Book Search service

Some of the methods that are common to all searchers are
setResultSetSize, clearResults, execute(query),
setSearchCompleteCallback, setUserDefinedLabel, and
setLinkTarget. The setResultSetSize method sets the number
of results returned by a searcher. The clearResults method clears the
search results and resets the searcher. The
setSearchCompleteCallback method registers a callback method
on the searcher to be invoked when the search completes. The
setUserDefinedLabel method sets a label for search result section,
which replaces the default label Local, Web, or Blog. The
setLinkTarget method specifies the link target for links in the search
results. The default is to open the links a new browser window.

The search control displays the query results for the different searchers
added to a search control object in one of the two draw modes: linear
or tabbed. The linear draw mode is the default and is shown in Fig.
10.3.

▶ Local (4)   ✿

▶ Web (6)

▶ Video (4)   ✿

▶ Blog (4)   ✿

▶ News (4)   ✿

▶ Book (4)

Fig. 10.3 Linear Draw Mode

The tabbed draw mode is shown in Fig. 10.4.

Fig. 10.4 Tabbed Draw Mode

The search results may be displayed in one of the three expansion modes: open, closed, or partial. In the open expansion mode the search results are displayed fully. In the closed mode the search results are not displayed until a UI element such as an arrow is clicked. The partial search result displays partial results. The default expansion mode is partial.

10.4 Creating a Google Ajax Web Search Application

In this section we shall create a Google Ajax Search application using the Google Local search service. To the *ajaxsearch.jsp* add the Google Ajax Search API JavaScript library. Specify the Google Ajax Search API key in the src attribute for the script tag.

```
<script
src="http://www.google.com/uds/api?file=uds.js&v=1.0&
key=ABQIAAAAItAEL-H-GuOHsDfD7Mxm1hSFcmgG4ILrfBhrLV-
hrgg2-UNeQhR4CSVn6vmsU_8IvmmjnIcWuaTufg"
type="text/javascript"></script>
```

Create a JavaScript function, onLoad(), to add a search control and search service. In the onLoad() function create a search control object.

```
var searchControl = new GSearchControl();
```

Set the result set size to GSearch.LARGE_RESULTSET, which typically returns 8 results.

```
searchControl.setResultSetSize(GSearch.LARGE_RESULTSE
T);
```

Create a GlocalSearch searcher object for the Google Local search service.

```
var localSearch = new GlocalSearch();
```

Add the searcher to the search control.

```
searchControl.addSearcher(localSearch);
```

Set the location for which the local search is to be performed with the `setCenterPoint(location)` method.

```
localSearch.setCenterPoint("Berlin Germany");
```

Create a `GdrawOptions` object to specify the draw options for the search results.

```
var drawOptions = new GdrawOptions();
```

Set the draw mode to `linear`.

```
drawOptions.setDrawMode(GSearchControl.DRAW_MODE_LINE
AR);
```

Specify a `div` element to display the search control results.

```
<div id="searchcontrol">Loading</div>
```

Activate the search control and display the results in the `searchcontrol` div.

```
searchControl.draw(document.getElementById("searchcon
trol"));
```

Register the `onLoad()` function with the document using the `setOnLoadCallback` static method of the `GSearch` class. When the document has completed loading the `onLoad()` function will get invoked.

```
GSearch.setOnLoadCallback(OnLoad);
```

The *ajaxsearch.jsp* is listed below.

```
<!DOCTYPE    HTML    PUBLIC    "-//W3C//DTD    HTML    4.01
Transitional//EN"
  "http://www.w3.org/TR/html4/loose.dtd">
  <%@  page  contentType="text/html;charset=windows-
1252"%>
  <html xmlns="http://www.w3.org/1999/xhtml">
    <head>
      <meta                    http-equiv="content-type"
      content="text/html; charset=utf-8"/>
      <title>Google AJAX Search</title>
      <link
      href="http://www.google.com/uds/css/gsearch.css"
      type="text/css" rel="stylesheet"/>
      <script
    src="http://www.google.com/uds/api?file=uds.js&v=1.
0&key=ABQIAAAAItAEL-H-GuOHsDfD7MxmlhSFcmgG4ILrfBhrLV-
hrgg2-UNeQhR4CSVn6vmsU_8IvmmjnIcWuaTufg"
```

```
type="text/javascript"></script>
<script language="Javascript" type="text/javascript">
    function OnLoad() {
    var searchControl = new GSearchControl();
 searchControl.setResultSetSize(GSearch.LARGE_RESULTS
ET);
        var localSearch = new GlocalSearch();
        searchControl.addSearcher(localSearch);
        localSearch.setCenterPoint("Berlin Germany");
var drawOptions = new GdrawOptions();
drawOptions.setDrawMode(GSearchControl.DRAW_MODE_LINE
AR);
searchControl.draw(document.getElementById("searchcon
trol",drawOptions));
        }
        GSearch.setOnLoadCallback(OnLoad);
        </script>
    </head>
    <body><div
id="searchcontrol">Loading</div></body>
    </html>
```

Copy the *ajaxsearch.jsp* to the *ajaxsearch.jsp* file in JDeveloper. Right-click on the *ajaxsearch.jsp* and select **Run** to run the JSP as shown in Fig. 10.5.

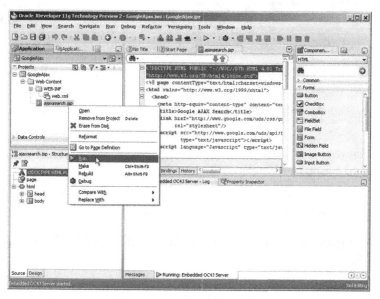

Fig. 10.5 Running Ajax Web Search Application

The Google Local search service page gets displayed. Specify a search term, for example "Universität", and click on **Search** as shown in Fig. 10.6. The Google Local search service searches only in the location specified by the setCenterPoint method of the GlocalSearch object.

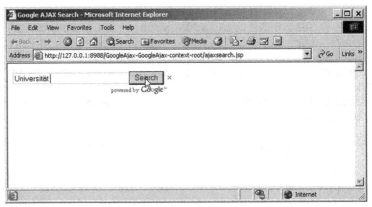

Fig. 10.6 Google Ajax Web Search

The search result gets displayed in expansion mode PARTIAL as shown in Fig. 10.7.

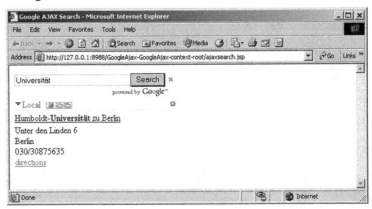

Fig. 10.7 Results of Google Ajax Web Search

To display all the search results click on show all results as shown in Fig. 10.8.

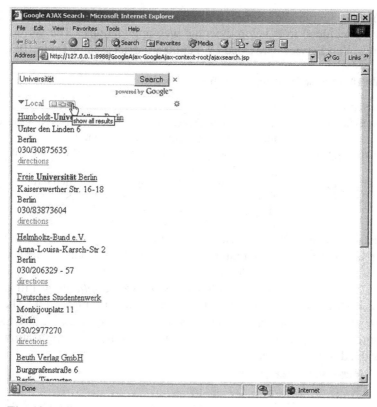

Fig. 10.8 All Search Results

10.5 Web Search with Yahoo Web Services

Asynchronous JavaScript and XML (Ajax) is a web technique to transfer XML data between a browser and a server without reloading the web page. Ajax is implemented using the XMLHttpRequest object. A limitation of XMLHttpRequest is that Ajax requests may be made only to the same web server that serves the web page from which the Ajax request is sent. If the web application is running on one server and the Web Service is on another server an XMLHttpRequest request does not get sent. Various methods are available to send an Ajax request to a remote server some of which are digitally signing your scripts and using an alternative XMLHttpRequest API. One of the methods, which we shall discuss in this chapter, is to use a proxy web server that routes Ajax requests from the web application to the Web Service.

Yahoo Search Web Services provides various services and content that may be included to develop dynamic web applications. The various Web Search Web Services provided by Yahoo are discussed in Table 10.3.

Table 10.3 Yahoo Web Search Web Services

Web Service	Description
Context Search	The contextual web search service returns web pages that match a query within a specified context.
Related Suggestion	Provides suggestions for related queries based on the submitted query.
Spelling Suggestion	Provides suggested spellings for a specified term.
Web Search	Provides a web search service using REST (Representational State Transfer).

Before Yahoo Web Service may be used, registration with Yahoo Search Web Services is required. To register with Yahoo Search Web Services   login   to   URL *http://search.yahooapis.com/webservices/register_application*. Fill out the Yahoo Developer Registration form as shown in Fig. 10.9. The web application URL in which Yahoo Search Web Services are accessed is required to be specified. The procedure to obtain the web application url is explained in the next section.

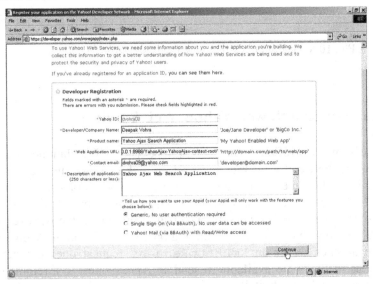

Fig. 10.9 Registering with Yahoo Search Web Services

When the registration form is submitted, Yahoo Search Web Services provides with an application id with which Yahoo Search Web Services may be accessed. Save a copy of the application id.

10.6 Creating an Ajax Web Search Application for Yahoo

First, create a JDeveloper application and project. Select **File>New** and in the **New Gallery** window select **General** in **Categories** and **Application** in **Items** and click on **OK**. In the **Create Application** window specify an **Application Name**, YahooAjax for example, and click on **OK**. In the **Create Project** window specify a **Project Name**, YahooAjax for example, and click on **OK**. Create a JSP file, *input.jsp*, in the project. Select **File>New** and in the **New Gallery** window select **Web Tier>JSP** in **Categories** and **JSP** in **Items** and click on **OK**. In the **Create JSP** window specify a file name and click on **OK**. A JSP gets added to the **Application Navigator** as shown in Fig. 10.10.

Fig. 10.10 Yahoo Ajax Web Search Application

The example JDeveloper application web application URL is http://127.0.0.1:8988/YahooAjax-YahooAjax-context-root/, which is to be specified in the **Web Application URL** field when registering with the Yahoo Search Web Services. To obtain the web application URL right-click on *input.jsp* and select **Run**.

In the web application we shall use the Contextual Web Search service to submit a context-base web search query. The request URL for

the   contextual   web   search   Web   Service   is
http://search.yahooapis.com/WebSearchService/V1/contextSearch. The
required request parameters to a contextual web search query are `appid`
and `context`. The value of the `appid` parameter is the application Id
provided by Yahoo Search Web Services and the `context` parameter
specifies the context string in which the web search query is sent. Some of
the commonly used request parameters are discussed in Table 10.4.

Table 10.4 Request Parameters

Parameter	Description
appid	Required parameter. Specifies the application id as a string.
query	Specifies the query string.
context	Required parameter. Specifies the context string.
results	Specifies the number of results to return. Default value is 10. Maximum value is 100.
start	Specifies the starting result position. Default value is 1.
format	Specifies the type of file to search for. Default value is "any". Other values that may be specifies are html, msword, pdf, ppt, rss, txt and xls.
output	Specifies the format of the output. Default value is xml. Other values may be json and php.
callback	For json output specifies the callback method for the JSON data.

The XML response returned by the Contextual Web Search service
conforms   to   the   XML   Schema
*http://search.yahooapis.com/WebSearchService/V1/WebSearchResponse.x
sd.* The response fields in the Web Service response are discussed in Table
10.5.

Table 10.5 Response Fields

Field	Description
ResultSet	The root element. Contains all the responses.
Result	The element for a response.
totalResultsAvailable	Number of query matches.
totalResultsReturned	Number of query matches returned.
firstResultPosition	Position of the first result.
Title	Title of a web page.
Summary	Summary of a web page returned.
Url	URL of the web page.
ClickUrl	URL for linking to the web page.
MimeType	MIME type of the page.
ModificationDate	The last modified date.
Cache	URL of the cached result.

In the *input.jsp* add a form containing fields for application id, query, results, and context. The form may be submitted using GET or POST, but to use a context with many search terms use the POST method. The form element is specified as follows.

```
<form name="requesturl"
action="http://search.yahooapis.com/WebSearchServic
e/V1/contextSearch"
method="POST">
```

The complete *input.jsp* is listed below.

```
<!DOCTYPE    HTML    PUBLIC    "-//W3C//DTD    HTML    4.01
Transitional//EN"
  "http://www.w3.org/TR/html4/loose.dtd">
<%@    page    contentType="text/html;charset=windows-
1252"%>
  <html>
      <head>
          <meta http-equiv="Content-Type"
          content="text/html; charset=windows-1252"/>
          <title>input</title>
      </head>
      <body><form name="requesturl"
action="http://search.yahooapis.com/WebSearchServic
e/V1/contextSearch" method="POST">
      <table>
        <tbody>
          <tr>
            <th>Contextual Web Search</th>
          </tr>
          <tr>
            <td>
   <input type="hidden" name="appid"
value="QwDUK7DV34H98YaFWsa3gHt.P68uPPI7ThU92omV19uT
85g9CAyqBUGmx.8eTF0-" readonly="readonly"/>
            </td>
          </tr>
          <tr>
            <td>
             <label>Query:</label>
            </td>
            <td>
             <input type="text" name="query"/>
            </td>
          </tr>
          <tr>
```

```
        <td>
         <label>Results:</label>
        </td>
        <td>
         <input type="text" name="results"/>
        </td>
       </tr>
       <tr>
        <td>
         <label for="context">Context:</label>
        </td>
        <td>
         <textarea      name="context"      cols="15"
         rows="3"></textarea>
        </td>
       </tr>
       <tr>
        <td>
         <input type="submit"/>
        </td>
       </tr>
      </tbody>
     </table>
   </form></body>
 </html>
```

Copy *input.jsp* listing to *input.jsp* in JDeveloper. To run the web application right-click on *input.jsp* and select **Run** as shown in Fig. 10.11.

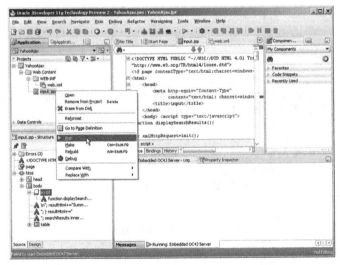

Fig. 10.11 Running Yahoo Search Web Services Application

The contextual web search form gets displayed. Specify a query term and one or more context terms and click on the **Submit Query** button as shown in Fig. 10.12.

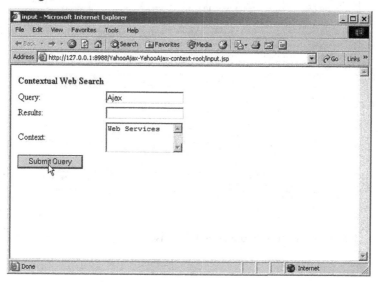

Fig. 10.12 Submitting a Query

The XML response returned by the Web Service gets displayed as shown in Fig. 10.13. The search results consist of the root element ResultSet, which contains Result elements for the different web pages returned by the Web Service. We have not yet used Ajax to send a web search query. We shall add Ajax to the contextual web search in the next section.

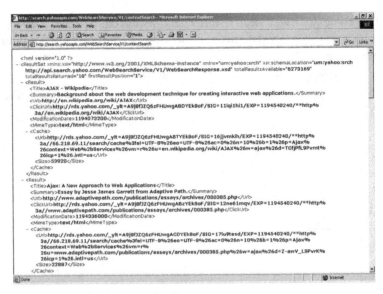

Fig. 10.13 Yahoo WebService Response

10.7 Sending an Ajax Request with Yahoo Search Web Services

To send an Ajax request we shall use a proxy servlet that routes the XMLHttpRequest from the browser to the Yahoo Web Service. If an XMLHttpRequest is sent without a proxy servlet the XMLHttpRequest does not get sent and an error gets generated.

```
Error: uncaught exception: Permission denied to call
method XMLHttpRequest.open
```

A proxy servlet may be developed or the HTTP proxy servlet[1] may be used. Download *httpProxyPackage.jar*. Add the proxy servlet JAR file to the **Libraries** of the YahooAjax project. To add a JAR file to the project select **Tools>Project Properties**. In the **Project Properties** window select **Libraries** and add the JAR file with **Add JAR/Directory** button. Click on **OK** in **Project Properties** window as shown in Fig. 10.14.

---

[1] HTTP Proxy Servlet- http://www.servletsuite.com/servlets/httpproxy.htm

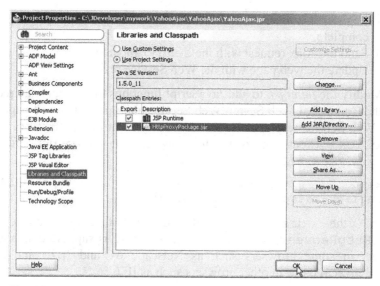

Fig. 10.14 Adding Proxy Servlet JAR File to Project Libraries

To the web.xml file add <servlet/> and <servlet-mapping/> elements for the proxy servlet following the description element.

```
<servlet>
    <servlet-name>HttpProxy</servlet-name>
    <servlet-
    class>com.jsos.httpproxy.HttpProxyServlet</servl
    et-class>
        <init-param>
            <param-name>host</param-name>
            <param-
    value>http://search.yahooapis.com/WebSearchServi
    ce/V1/contextSearch</param-value>
        </init-param>
</servlet>
<servlet-mapping>
    <servlet-name>HttpProxy</servlet-name>
    <url-pattern>/servlet/yahoo</url-pattern>
</servlet-mapping>
```

The procedure to send an Ajax request is as follows.

1. Initiate an Ajax request from an HTML event such as a button click.
2. Create an XMLHttpRequest object.
3. Open a connection with the Web Service URL using the open() method of the XMLHttpRequest object.

4. Register a callback function to be invoked when the Ajax request is complete.
5. Send the Ajax request with the `send()` method.
6. Update the web page with the Web Service response.

Modify the *input.jsp* to add JavaScript functions to send an Ajax request to the Contextual Web Search Web Service and update the web page with the Web Service response. To the `input` element of type `button` add a `onclick` event handler to invoke a JavaScript function `displaySearchResults()`.

```
<input                                    type="SUBMIT"
onclick="displaySearchResults()"/>
```

In the `displaySearchResults` function create an `XMLHttpRequest` object. `XMLHttpRequest` is supported as a native object in some browsers such as Netscape 6+ and IE7 and as an `ActiveXObject` in other browsers such as IE 6.

```
var xmlHttpRequest=init();
  function init(){
if (window.XMLHttpRequest) {
   return new XMLHttpRequest();
   } else if (window.ActiveXObject) {
    return new ActiveXObject("Microsoft.XMLHTTP");
   }
}
```

Specify the proxy servlet URL to which an Ajax request is to be sent. Obtain the values for query, results and context request parameters from the input form. Encode the request parameter values using the `encodeURI` method.

```
var
url="servlet/yahoo?appid=QwDUK7DV34H98YaFWsa3gHt.P68u
PPI7ThU92omV19uT85g9CAyqBUGmx.8eTF0-"+
   "&query="+encodeURI(document.getElementById("query"
).value)+
   "&results="+encodeURI(document.getElementById("resu
lts").value)+
   "&context="+encodeURI(document.getElementById("cont
ext").value);
```

Open an `XMLHttpRquest` request using the `open()` method. If few context terms are to be used the `GET` method may be used. Specify the third parameter of the `open()` method as `true` for asynchronous requests.

```
xmlHttpRequest.open("GET", url, true);
```

Register a callback function that is to be invoked when the request state changes using the onreadystatechange property of the XMLHttpRequest object.

```
xmlHttpRequest.onreadystatechange=processRequest;
```

Send the XMLHttpRequest request using the send() method with null as the parameter to the method, the request method being GET.

```
xmlHttpRequest.send(null);
```

In the callback function check if the request is complete and the request status is "OK" and invoke the JavaScript function processResponse() to update the web page with the Web Service response. A readyState value of 4 corresponds to a completed request and HTTP status code 200 corresponds to "OK" request status.

```
if(xmlHttpRequest.readyState==4){
   if(xmlHttpRequest.status==200){
      processResponse();
   }
 }
}
```

To the input form add a <div/> element searchResults to display the search results. In the processResponse function obtain the XML response with the responseXML attribute of the XMLHttpRequest object.

```
var xmlMessage=xmlHttpRequest.responseXML;
```

Next, update the searchResults div with the Web Service response. Retrieve the searchResults element with getElementById method.

```
var
searchResults=document.getElementById("searchResults"
);
```

Construct an HTML string with which to update the searchResults div. We shall display the search results as an ordered list.

```
var resultHtml="<ol>";
```

Obtain the node list of the Result elements in the Web Service response using the getElementsByTagName() method. Each of the Result elements contains a web page returned by the Web Service.

```
var
resultList=xmlMessage.getElementsByTagName("Result");
```

Iterate over the result set to construct the HTML string to update the web page with. We shall display the web page title, the URL to the web page and a summary of the web page.

```
var len =resultList.length;
for(var i=0; i<len;i++){
var result=resultList[i];
var
title=result.getElementsByTagName("Title")[0].first
Child.nodeValue;
var
summary=result.getElementsByTagName("Summary")[0].f
irstChild.nodeValue;
var
url=result.getElementsByTagName("Url")[0].firstChil
d.nodeValue;

resultHtml+="<li>Title:"+"<a         href=\""+url+"\">"
+title+ "</a></li>\n";
resultHtml+="Summary: "+summary+"</li>";
}
resultHtml+="</ol>";
```

Set the value of the `searchResults` `<div/>` as the string constructed from the Web Service response.

```
searchResults.innerHTML=resultHtml;
```

The complete *input.jsp* is listed below.

```
<!DOCTYPE HTML PUBLIC "-//W3C//DTD HTML 4.01
Transitional//EN"
"http://www.w3.org/TR/html4/loose.dtd">
<%@ page contentType="text/html;charset=windows-
1252"%>
<html>
    <head>
        <meta http-equiv="Content-Type"
            content="text/html; charset=windows-1252"/>
        <title>input</title>
    </head>
    <body> <script type="text/javascript">
function displaySearchResults(){
var xmlHttpRequest=init();
function init(){
```

```
if (window.XMLHttpRequest) {
            return new XMLHttpRequest();
} else if (window.ActiveXObject) {
  return new ActiveXObject("Microsoft.XMLHTTP");
  }
}
var
url="servlet/yahoo?appid=QwDUK7DV34H98YaFWsa3gHt.P68u
PPI7ThU92omV19uT85g9CAyqBUGmx.8eTF0-"+
"&query="+encodeURI(document.getElementById("query").
value)+
"&results="+encodeURI(document.getElementById("result
s").value)+
"&context="+encodeURI(document.getElementById("contex
t").value);
xmlHttpRequest.open("GET", url, true);
xmlHttpRequest.onreadystatechange=processRequest;
xmlHttpRequest.send(null);
function processRequest(){
if(xmlHttpRequest.readyState==4){
   if(xmlHttpRequest.status==200){
      processResponse();
   }
  }
}
function processResponse(){
var xmlMessage=xmlHttpRequest.responseXML;
var
searchResults=document.getElementById("searchResults"
);
var resultHtml="<ol>";
var
resultList=xmlMessage.getElementsByTagName("Result");
var len =resultList.length;
for(var i=0; i<len;i++){
var result=resultList[i];
var
title=result.getElementsByTagName("Title")[0].firstCh
ild.nodeValue;
var
summary=result.getElementsByTagName("Summary")[0].fir
stChild.nodeValue;
var
url=result.getElementsByTagName("Url")[0].firstChild.
nodeValue;
resultHtml+="<li>Title:"+"<a         href=\""+url+"\">"
+title+ "</a></li>\n";
```

```
resultHtml+="Summary: "+summary+"</li>";
}
resultHtml+="</ol>";
searchResults.innerHTML=resultHtml;
 }
}
</script>
<table>
  <tbody>
    <tr>
      <th>Contextual Web Search</th>
    </tr>
    <tr>
      <td>
        <label>Query:</label>
      </td>
      <td>
        <input type="text" id="query"/>
      </td>
    </tr>
    <tr>
      <td>
        <label>Results:</label>
      </td>
      <td>
        <input type="text" id="results"/>
      </td>
    </tr>
    <tr>
      <td>
        <label>Context:</label>
      </td>
      <td>
        <textarea id="context" cols="15" rows="3">
        </textarea>
      </td>
    </tr>
    <tr>
      <td>
        <input                          type="SUBMIT"
        onclick="displaySearchResults()"/>
      </td>
    </tr>
    <tr>
      <td>
        <div id="searchResults"></div>
      </td>
```

```
    </tr>
    </tbody>
  </table></body>
</html>
```

10.8 Running the Yahoo Ajax Web Search Application

Next, we shall run the Ajax web application to send a query using Ajax an update the web page with the query response. Right-click on *input.jsp* and select **Run** as shown in Fig. 10.15.

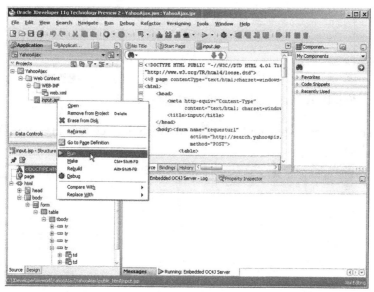

Fig. 10.15 Running Yahoo Ajax Web Search Application

In the web search form specify a query term and a context term. As an example search for the term "Ajax" in the context of "WebServices". Click on the **Submit Query** button as shown in Fig. 10.16.

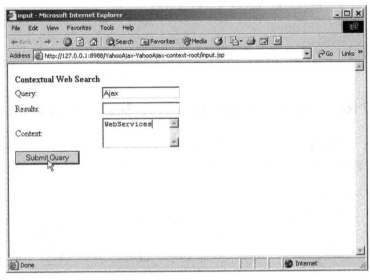

Fig. 10.16 Yahoo Ajax Contextual Web Search

The web page gets updated with the Web Service response as shown in Fig. 10.17.

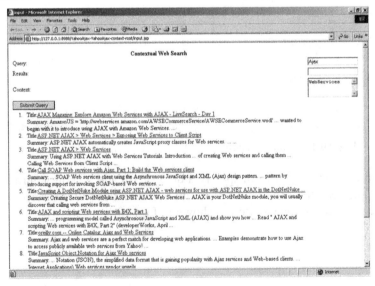

Fig. 10.17 Results of Yahoo Contextual Web Search

More than one context terms may be specified and the number of results to be returned may also be specified. As an example specify results as 5 and specify context terms as "WebServices", "XML", and "WSDL" for query term "Ajax". The specified number of web pages get displayed for the context based web search as shown in Fig. 10.18.

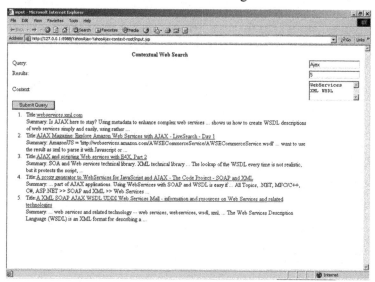

Fig. 10.18 Results of Yahoo Contextual Web Search with Multiple Terms

10.9 Summary

Ajax may be added to web search using the Google Ajax Search API and the Yahoo Search Web Services. In this chapter we created a web search application using the Google Local search service to web search a specified location. We also used the Yahoo Search Web Services Contextual Web search service to web search using contextual terms.

Sources of Information

- W3C XMLHttpRequest Specification-
  http://www.w3.org/TR/XMLHttpRequest/
- Oracle Jdeveloper 11g-
  http://www.oracle.com/technology/products/jdev/11/index.html
- Prototype JavaScript Framework- http://www.prototypejs.org/
- Google Web Toolkit- http://code.google.com/webtoolkit/
- Direct Web Remoting- http://getahead.org/dwr
- AjaxTags- http://ajaxtags.sourceforge.net/
- JBoss Ajax4jsf- http://www.jboss.org/projects/jbossajax4jsf
- Xajax- http://www.xajaxproject.org/
- Google AJAX Feed API- http://code.google.com/apis/ajaxfeeds/
- Google AJAX Search API- http://code.google.com/apis/ajaxsearch/
- Yahoo Search Web Services- http://developer.yahoo.com/search/

Index